CHRIST WITHIN ME

by

George Simms
Archbishop of Armagh

FOREWORD
by
William Cardinal Conway

Christian Journals Limited
Belfast

First published January 1975 by Christian Journals Limited, 2 Bristow Park, Belfast BT9 6TH.

ISBN 0 904302 10 5

Cover by Phyllis Arnold

FILMSET BY DOYLE PHOTOSETTING LTD., TULLAMORE, IRELAND.

Printed in Ireland

CONTENTS

FOREWORD

Lent is primarily a period of preparation—preparation to celebrate the paschal mystery of Our Lord's passion, death and resurrection, during Holy Week, preparation ultimately for our own death and resurrection.

In the early Church this theme of preparation was very clear. Lent was the forty-day period when penitents got ready for reconciliation with the Church on Holy Thursday and Catechumens prepared for their baptism during the Easter Vigil. Inevitably, and very early, it came to be seen as a period of preparation for all of us.

Thinking—or 'reflection', 'meditation'—is an important element in the life of the Christian and particularly during the Lenten period. I remember when I was a boy priests 'giving a mission' often took as their opening text the words "With desolation is the whole land made desolate because there is no man who thinketh in his heart" and without wishing to overstress the 'desolation' one can readily agree that periods of 'thinking things out' are good for the soul. Archbishop Simms' book is well calculated to help this process during the Lenten period. It is written in a quiet reflective mood and like all good reflection it is circular rather than linear in its thought, coming back again and again to the same important truths of Christian living, looking at them from different points of view and in different contexts, and all the time winning acceptance by its gentle persuasiveness. The extract from the "Breastplate of St. Patrick" provides a fitting framework for these meditations and although written in a period far removed from our own its relevance to the world of our day is sometimes quite startling. This is a book which will help to set the wheels of reflection turning, gently but effectively.

+ William Cardinal Conway

17th December, 1974.

Chapter 1

Introducing Lent

We are right to approach Lent sensitively, without ostentation. This official season of penitence draws from us personal decisions and hidden action. A self-conscious Lent defeats its own ends. A joyful Lent is more likely to be spiritually fruitful.

Joy and discipline do not exclude each other. There is ecstasy in endurance. There is triumph in control. Action which craves for no public recognition can bring a special inward happiness of its own. Achievement which looks for no applause becomes our business.

Jesus said 'when you fast', not 'if you fast'. He counted among the features of truly human conduct such qualities as: restraint, discipline, control, purity of motive, and a zest for research in the hidden things of the spirit. The 'when' suggests that time must be found for pruning wherever there is growth, for fasting wherever diet and appetite are involved, for silence among the talkative, for withdrawal by the gregarious. The 'if' would have left the matter too vague; the soul's pulse can easily start to beat irregularly, the good works too often run down. The organised life of a penitential season provides impetus for the individual at a delicate moment, of which the less said the better, and the more done the healthier.

'When you fast', said Jesus Christ, 'anoint your head'.* The anointing for the Jew was not unlike a garlanding for the Greek; it suggested gaiety and joy. Our Lord's Lent, if we dare to call those days he spent in the wilderness by such a name, was spent apart in lonely combat. His discipline was not exercised before men to be seen of them or to be praised by them. As has been strikingly said, 'Jesus showed his wounds only to God'. The world saw the fruits of his life, not the seeds. In loneliness he endured the struggle. Among those he loved and served he displayed strength, not agony; healing and not wounds. His suffering and inner struggles were in the dark of Gethsemane and on the barren site of Calvary. His crucifixion was lonely; his resurrection was with others. He still brings many back to life.

An early Christian conversation, held in the deserts of North Africa, lies behind the familiar custom of choosing a book for Lenten reading. A young disciple, gone stale at his prayers, turns to one of his elders in the community and says: 'Give me a word that I may live.'† He was obviously hungry for new thoughts about his faith. There followed a spiritual discourse. Then, through reading and turning over thoughts in conversation, truths about God and man were grasped afresh and made alive again. The listener was learning about prayer and life by lending an attentive ear to what was spoken. He found that discussion and questioning drew him into the conversation and the fellowship. His own

*Matthew, 6, 17.
†John Cassian, Collations.

7

thinking and the observations he was able to make contributed to the spiritual discoveries shared by the whole company. In this way the inner life was nourished. The longings of the heart found an outlet. Ordinary, familiar words remained simple, but also acquired new depth. Lenten reading is best seen as a combined operation.

The urgency of feeding the minds in a world of people, both literate and illiterate, is clear. The season of Lent for the Christian is a time for such nourishment. Too often the long weeks before Easter have suggested leanness and a bleak atmosphere of discipline by prohibitions. The forty days provide an opportunity for everyone, whatever stage of spiritual development he may have reached, to read and to pray, to tell stories and join in discussions, to share thoughts and to make fresh contacts with people and life. The background of quiet supplied a spiritual in-service and those who embarked upon the course became remarkably relaxed and much more at ease with those whom they were to meet in future in the world. Helen Waddell* wrote of the Christian athletes and heroes who searched for God through prayer and study and in so doing discovered themselves: 'They go out into the desert not to escape people but to learn how to find them'.

The Breastplate

The phrases from a portion of Saint Patrick's Breastplate will be studied, discussed, applied to life, and used as headlines for our praying and thinking in the pages that follow.

The words translated from the Irish by Cecil Frances Alexander, the celebrated hymn-writer, were first used on St. Patrick's day, March 17th 1889. Since then, they

*The Desert Fathers.

have become increasingly familiar, not only in Ireland, but across the world.

It is not surprising, therefore, that among the prayers chosen by the churches in Ireland for their appointed day of 'intercession for peace' on Sunday, 30th September 1973 this popular verse was printed on the widely circulated leaflet for use throughout Ireland, in open spaces, in market-squares, and in many kinds of meeting places. Those who gathered, in thousands, or in hundreds, or in smaller groups from many traditions and backgrounds joined with a single longing as they said or sang:

> Christ be with me, Christ within me,
> Christ behind me, Christ before me,
> Christ beside me, Christ to win me,
> Christ to comfort and restore me.
>
> Christ beneath me, Christ above me,
> Christ in quiet, Christ in danger,
> Christ in hearts of all that love me,
> Christ in mouth of friend and stranger.

The name of 'breastplate' given to this prayer sounds at first too protective for an adventurous Christian to wear. However, the positive tone and the direct approach of the words catch the spirit of the days of the fifth-century saint and are not lacking in initiative and enterprise.

The prayer, it is agreed, dates from a period later than Patrick's time. Yet it echoes much of the conviction and resolve of the saint's autobiography, by name *The Confession*; a document that contains a moving personal testimony and attracts us with its honesty and candour. The words of the prayer under examination belong to every period and age; in a sense they are timeless; they refuse to be out-dated and serve Christians, in whatever predicament they find themselves, as world-prayers.

Accordingly, we will attempt to take the phrases as headlines for our own thinking. There is something creative about doing a season of meditating, contemplating, and plain thinking. Such a programme sounds deceptively peaceful; it can, in fact, be both a disturbing experience and a strenuous exercise.

A sharing, however, of the spiritual discoveries made by Christians in an Ireland of long ago ought not to be unfruitful. At least, we will become aware of prayers and thoughts that have lasted and have been sternly tested. The simple, yet profound words from those days have still something to say to us. They live, because Christ, their theme, lives.

We often find that spiritual history repeats the moods and yearnings of ordinary human beings through each succeeding century. Their sins are not new, nor are their spiritual discoveries necessarily bigger and better.

Sometimes we try to compose prayers of our own; often we find comfort in new prayers to match contemporary needs and wishes. We also turn to favourite prayers from the treasury of Christian worship and find a touch of kinship with those whose approach to life and cast of mind are reflected in the time-honoured phrases.

The mind behind the Breastplate prayer was shaped and influenced by the events in the life of Jesus Christ. The prayer can help us to return to that life, to bridge the gaps that bewilderment, spiritual weariness and sheer neglect have caused. Such a prayer can help us to grow in spirit.

The poetry of the words, the repeated refrain in line

10

upon line, the very shape of this gem of devotion bring an urgency and a keen insistence to the business of praying. Half a hymn and half a litany, the whole verse reminds us that 'to live is Christ'. To be Christian is to have a relationship with Him that so fully commits us that a response from our whole being is demanded. This relationship with Christ covers every human relationship.

This prayer seeks Christ's presence and companionship in all the events and activities of the day. It brings life back to those who are apathetic, indifferent, sleepy, only partly alive, or else plain sinful. Starting as one man's prayer, it soon became a community prayer, a family prayer, a prayer of the church, a prayer, used by those Christians, who sensed that for all their divisions and differences, they were one in Christ.

There is movement and progress in the prayer. Each phrase forms a link and so lengthens our responsibilities as we pray through to the end. Those who penned the beautiful manuscripts in that golden period of Celtic Christian art and learning pictured themselves on a journey, the lines between which they wrote, carefully controlling the letters and lovingly cherishing each word, were like paths on a journey which had twists and turns. The goal was God, for their work was their way into God.

Lenten Journey

On the threshold of Lent, the Christian faces a spiritual journey. For Jesus the road to Jerusalem led not merely to a city but to a crucifixion; he had a clear and firm purpose in heading for that direction. What happened on the way seemed to show that his journey was really necessary. There were issues to be faced and decisions to be made; they could not be by-passed. Prophecy was fulfilled as he travelled and the traveller became known to the companions who shared his journey.

The way of Christian living and believing has often been described in terms of travel. The whole person becomes involved in the process of walking and other far speedier modes of progress from place to place; he cannot leave part of himself behind. A spiritual journey in Lent also makes demands on the whole person; it is not exclusively planned for private soul-making and merely individual renewal. Others around us have a place on the road. This season of prayer and thought and decision-making is a community event; it has social overtones. In this way, many joining together and acting in partnership can be set on the route to the place where decisions have to be made and suffering can scarcely be avoided.

If we move together as fellow-Christians into the mood of Lent, with a spirit of sharing, of giving and giving up, with a readiness to serve a world in need, we will have, to our surprise, a new-found joy in discovering what life is all about. It will be strange, too, if we do not stumble on some unforeseen adventures on the way. The joy will lie more in the experience than in any particular achievement.

Some such spirit of adventure in the faith was captured when Jesus approached the city of Jericho on one of his recorded journeyings, and met a blind man sitting by the side of the road, begging. There appeared to be nothing accidental, or merely incidental, about this encounter. The interruption, the subsequent conversation and the whole scene fit perfectly into the whole travel story. The blind man, who shouts 'Son of David' in a phrase that has more point in it than the bystanders realise, catches the attention of Jesus passing by, and shows in spite of his blindness a keen perception of what is happening all around him. The people, on the other hand, who resent this beggarly intrusion and look upon the incident as a nuisance and a hazard, demonstrate their own blindness. They attempt to stifle the cries for help and to intercept the protests. Jesus, however, turned the occasion into an illustration of his journey's purpose. His healing of blind Bartimaeus was more than a benevolent aside as he passed by; it was clearly an integral part of the good news which the traveller was spreading about the kingdom of God in a world of needy people.

We embark upon a Lenten journey through these pages that follow in another year of uncertainties and anxieties. As we pray and think about the events on the way and our manner of approaching them, we will increase our awareness of some very human issues, close to our hearts; we will waken up to the importance of other problems, not so close to us, which up to now have not troubled us. To face them and to see them as part of the experience of living and serving in our world is a Christian responsibility. We do well not to shut our eyes to those whom we meet or pass by on the road; nor are we right to look the other way when incidents take place and danger-spots are reached, in the hope that all can be glossed over and ignored. Growth in the spirit is found as often in the places where the traffic is thickest and the speed is checked, as in the lonely stretches of bog-land and the quiet seclusion of a peaceful country walk.

The long-term demands of this period of training need not be daunting, for growth in the spirit takes time.

Forty serves as a rough, round number as we calculate the length of Lent in days. We in this part of the world generally make our ready reckoning in hundreds. The people of the Bible often thought in 'forties'. Forty of anything suggested something sizable. Forty years of peace was bliss in a war-torn holy land; forty years long in the wilderness demanded endurance of a high order from the faithful on their long trek in the teeth of opposition and provocation. Forty days of temptation were times of genuine struggle and testing that required sustained acts of patience and a long-term faith. To be tempted to do the wrong thing or to make a disastrous, irrevocable choice may be the impulsive experience of an unguarded moment that is easily shrugged off and lightly forgotten; but to act faithfully, without flinching and often without recognition, for days upon end in surroundings of constant strain requires an inner discipline of a high order and demands deep reserves of grace.

The forty days which lay between the resurrection and the ascension of Jesus supplied the answers to the questions put to him by the tempter at the beginning in the loneliness of the wilderness. It took time and adversity for the truth to penetrate and for the glory of it to be revealed. Jesus looked back on all that had happened and showed that the scriptures had been fulfilled. There was no accident about his life; nor are Christian saints made by accident.

So day by day and week by week, either in private reading or in a fellowship of prayer and conversation this small book attempts to offer a time-table for the modest study of a large theme. A chapter for each week is suggested for private personal reading or for group discussion.

Lent need not be a dead season nor yet a dull one. It is after all concerned with life—your life and other people's lives. We must not look for sudden results. 'Take no thought of the harvest' wrote the poet, 'but only of proper sowing'.* There is much in our lives that needs time for growth, much that must for a while remain underground and hidden. Lent is misleadingly quiet; let it never be negative.

Nor is the season appointed as a time for self-centredness. Nothing could be further from the truth. It is supremely a time for others. 'Fasting and abstinence', wrote Massey Shepherd,† 'increase our capacity to give generously to the needs of those less fortunate than ourselves. Prayer enlarges our sensitivity to God's loving concern for all his creatures and serious study makes us more able to communicate our faith by word and deed in all our day-to-day work and relationships'.

A Spiritual Experience

Patrick in the intimate account of his faith and life indicates that there is little about which he can boast. 'Patrick the sinner'; in such terms he describes himself. There is nothing mealy-mouthed or falsely humble in the phrase. The note of protest and challenge sounds more frequently than we might expect as he writes on. We are fortunate to have two documents surviving; scholars generally are in agreement that the *Confession* and the *Letter to the soldiers of Coroticus* are from the pen of Patrick. They give us glimpses of a human personality very much alive. They help us to capture something of the faith and inspiration of what became a triumphant life. Yet Patrick was far from turning triumphalistic.

*T. S. Eliot, The Rock.
†Make His Name Glorious (California 1964).

15

The Christian faith is understood more clearly by us all when expressed in human lives. The doctrine of Christ's incarnation—the Word becoming flesh—may sound in the ears of the vigorous activist young citizen and for many another, as something technical, remote, and even forbidding. Yet the concerns that flow from incarnation-faith include care for the poor and oppressed, reverence for people's lives, equal justice for all regardless of race, colour or creed. This was a faith that found and still finds God in Christ, the Christ who 'though he was rich, became poor, that we through his poverty might be rich'.

The preaching of Patrick the sinner was patently practical: his love for people fills his writings. He moved among those who were in need of light and love and life. He had a driving force behind him.

The modern ring in his use of scripture makes some of his expressions sound intimate and homely. His style of applying his faith to every-day life with a personal slant and a lively spontaneity helps to convince us that here is a religion that supplies human needs, whatever the state of civilisation, however sophisticated the progress in technical discovery and achievement. When he describes his work of welfare through personal caring and evangelising as 'hunting and fishing', we smile. The picture words of the Hebrew psalm or the Irish countryside introduce the note of realism we are looking for. We smile, we do not scoff, for in terms of the rustic life in which he found himself, he searched people out and followed up his contacts with them, in a burning desire to banish ignorance and to free them from the fears of prejudice and superstition.

Patrick quotes St. Paul's letters with great frequency when he writes his own. The parallels bring to life all that he has read from the New Testament. The portrait of 'the slave of Christ' is vivid and poignant for him who had found tyranny and persecution uncomfortably near; the slave, 'bringing every thought into captivity to the obedience of Christ' was ready to surrender some of his freedoms. The fierce times, in which Patrick lived, served to demonstrate the strength of Christ's pity and the victorious quality of his compassion.

We still need this kind of presentation of a living faith. The fears without and within, which we all too frequently feel, can only be overcome by a practising faith that finds God at work in the world, in the very trouble spots and danger zones which so many, unthinking and mistrusting, imagine that He has deserted, as if God had abandoned us and withdrawn his protection. The false beliefs of Patrick's time and the so-called knowledge of his opponents were dealt with by a robust humility. This humble approach involved a showing up of his own weaknesses and an exposure of his personal problems. If ever there was a living example to demonstrate the truth of the phrase 'when I am weak, then am I strong',* Patrick the sinner provided it. His life was triumphant because he gave God the glory and the victory.

*2 Corinthians 12, 10.

17

Chapter 2

Christ Be With Me
Christ Within Me

For all its simplicity the *Christ be with me* stanza from St. Patrick's Breastplate matches in a remarkable way the spiritual experiences of this rather complicated saint. Composed years after Patrick's lifetime, the Breastplate serves as a compelling and convincing devotional commentary on the life of one who had a varied and effective pilgrimage. We find its words strangely modern and warmly human. They come to our rescue in all our problems.

Christ be with me recalls the loneliness on the hillslopes of Slemish in County Antrim, where the boy Patrick was on duty, watching over the animals as they fed. Far from home, with the status of a slave, Christ was with him; on the surface, however, the boy admitted that he was agnostic.

Christ within me penetrates more deeply. This large petition helps the unbeliever who for a time abandoned the faith of his upbringing. Patrick wrote in his Confession: 'I did not believe, I forsook God and did not keep his commandments'. His very awareness of such scepticism proved to be a turning point on his spiritual pilgrimage. Inner conviction and the power of the Spirit supplied him with courage for the next step out of slavery.

Christ behind me, Christ before me: these are words of trust in a shifty, superstitious environment of spiritism and wizardry. Patrick's faith was not daunted by the fear of what might tread behind him in the darkness. The presence of God through the youthful vision that came to him beset him 'behind and before'. True faith replaced crude superstition.

Christ beside me. This was a prayer offered at a time for decision-making. When Patrick was brought before kings and stood to face his trial, Christ at his side gave him the answers and supplied him with courage.

Christ to win me. In his ready response to a clearly heard call, Patrick won victories over himself. He overcame his own waywardness and triumphed over his enemies. He knew, however, that there was no credit to be claimed by him here. Not he, but the Christ that lived in him, was the conqueror.

Christ to comfort and restore me. He prayed in times of grim depression. His conscience often smote him. He has described his spiritual state in such bold and vivid terms as these: 'before I was afflicted, I was like a stone lying in the deep mire, and He that is mighty came, and in His mercy lifted me up, and indeed raised me aloft and placed me on top of the wall'. With God's help, he ceased to be a displaced person and a lost soul.

Christ beneath me, Christ above me. The words today would suit a prayer for air-travel, for space-men. They served the wandering Patrick, who compassed land and sea. His escape from Ireland was turned by faith into a journey with a purpose. He discovered that he had not run away but had been called to embark upon a voyage of exploration. Taking the wings of the morning, he found that, even in the uttermost parts of the sea, God was leading him.

Christ in quiet, Christ in danger. Such are the contrasts in a life of prayer and action. His time spent abroad, his returning and his communing with God in his heart, all these were essential parts of Patrick's life of service. Prayer preceded action; for him it was a priority.

Christ in hearts of all that love me: this he would exclaim as he founded a beloved community in a land of many afflictions. There, in a fellowship of faith and suffering, he came to know in a new way the Christ whose faith he had inherited from his parents.

Christ in mouth of friend and stranger: the words enshrine the missionary-hearted experience of Patrick, who like St. Paul, was all things to all men, whether they were bond or free, Jew or Greek. Both of these Christian leaders believed in meeting people half-way. The readiness to become servant of all, and to become weak in order to gain the weak appeared to be characteristic of both these Christian leaders.

Christ be with me

This a prayer for those who have lost touch with **God**. It serves as a starting point when prayers have **been** abandoned or neglected. 'Christ be with me' is **a cry** from the heart in the face of the anguish of spiritual, **and** even physical, emptiness.

The boy Patrick felt unwanted. He thought of himself as a mere unit in a slave gang, burdened with a task that was bleak and dispiriting. There seemed little hope of a change or relief; no new turn of fortune looked at all likely. Yet in the very atmosphere of misery and despair, there came to him a heartening vision of what he might do and be in the future. This was the realisation that someone cared; he sensed that he was loved by God and wanted by Him for a very different purpose, yet to be specified.

The incident provides an excellent example to give us encouragement when things seem to go constantly against us. We are swift to blame 'circumstances' and to become fatalistic about repeated misfortunes and disappointments. We need to learn the more elusive lesson that 'relationships' far more often than 'circumstances' require attention and improving. Our attitude to dangers and disasters can bring courage and faith to bear upon the most unpromising situations. Patrick broke away from his plight and predicament for new work, because his new relationship with God in Christ enabled him to venture into the unknown. Doubtless, sufferings and dangers would lie in the future no less than in the loneliness of the mountain as a slave-boy, but life was changed and he found a new meaning in living.

This urgent, pressing prayer 'Christ be with me' is more than a cry for help. It makes demands at all times, both in prosperity and in adversity. The initial turning to Christ may have come at a moment well remembered accurately recorded; the change and the break may have been shattering and revolutionary. The prayer, however, expects a follow-up and invites a response from us to all that Christ offers. The continued relationship is all-important. Believing includes belonging. He is ready to be with us always. Being a Christian is often described as life 'in Christ'.

Prayer has been commonly defined as 'being with God'. Prayer is a mood, a meeting, an approach, a kind of life; we miss much of its meaning, if we think only of prayer as a form of words. If we find praying a difficult and frustrating exercise at times, we do well to look to our own attitudes and moods. If there is nothing we can say, it may well be that we should be listening and not chafing. If our troubled and rebellious selves are too much to the forefront in our thoughts, then the words 'Christ be with me come to the rescue. It is not necessarily by change of wording nor by alteration of method that we will find ourselves progressing in the work of prayer with our situation improving. It is our relationship with God which claims prior attention.

Early Christians would often speak of the three stages through which the learner must pass in his course of prayer. He found himself first as a slave, praying through fear, in a panic; then as a hired servant, praying for rewards and returns; finally, as a son, praying for the love of it.

There is more of the slave-mentality in us when at prayer than we are willing to admit. If we have ignored the Almighty for much of the time when we have not felt his power and presence, on other occasions we find Him terrifyingly near. Prayer in such circumstances all too easily turns into an exercise in appeasement, born of fear. The relationship of slave to tyrant encourages a fawning flattery, a poor substitute for sincere and honest praise, free from mixed motives. Blind obedience is scarcely prayerful response. Requests that seek escape from danger and judgement and nothing

22

else are not worthy of the name of devotion. These cries from the heart, uttered through fear and trapped reactions, savour of the magic spell that wards off the evil eye with a shout or a flourish. Superstition keeps its gods far away with gifts and secret symbols.

The hireling's prayer works for results. Too often our petitions are mechanical. We insert them, as it were, in the appropriate slots for the withdrawal of the required answers. Such prayer seems to bargain with God; no conversation here, little patient waiting, only an official, business-like, almost professional relationship. We ask for God's bounty, his rewards; we do not stay to ask for God himself. As has been said, if we turn the other cheek in a conflict and do not gain the desired result, we become indignant that we should be obliged to turn the other cheek again . . . . and again. Prayer of this sort is taken up in an emergency and then dropped when it and all else fail. The hireling goes on strike; he has given up praying since he found it did not pay.

The son, however, has a relationship which has been his inheritance from the start of life. Prayer began in him ever since he belonged and was loved. If the son makes no response, he is still a son. If he says little and does less, the relationship with the Father is still there and holding. This state of affairs is not designed to encourage idleness or irresponsibility since the relationship relies on lively contact, communication, and working together. Otherwise, growth and maturing will be arrested, and the relationship will be starved of love and life.

Growth and maturing come through the companionship of prayer. Withdrawing in order to be with Christ is a discipline in itself. Time off for prayer must be rescued from the pressures of routine. Self-denial is a prelude to new affirmations about ourselves and life with God. To disengage from much that is trivial and petty is a needful preliminary to a re-engagement with all the claims that the world makes upon us. To withdraw from what has been destructive and poisonous in our hearts and minds is to be at once refreshed and invigorated by the influences of love and forgiveness in Christ's presence.

It seems, for example, a simple matter to end our prayers with the oft-repeated phrase 'through Jesus Christ our Lord'. Yet we make an elementary mistake if we think that this conventional ending will lend authenticity to any and every wild and selfish request. The time-honoured conclusion to the formal Christian prayer is open to abuse. We do better to treat this ending as a climax; for it is supremely through Christ that requests, petitions, and desires must be channeled. He receives all our prayers and sifts them. He joins our prayers with His. Thus our feeble and unworthy utterances are submitted to His testing; they are brought into harmony with His wishes and purposes and made consistent with His character.

In a still fuller traditional ending for a prayer, the part played by the living Christ, who is the same yesterday, today, and for ever, is underlined. 'Through Jesus Christ our Lord who lives and reigns with the Father and the Holy Spirit, ever one God, world without end': this more elaborate climax helps us to appreciate that the feeblest and least worthy prayer can be joined in solidarity to the body of the Christ who ever lives to make intercession. These prayers of ours may be personal, but they are not private; nor are they limited.

The risen Lord showed the power of his endless life amongst us. He met Mary Magdalene and brought reconciliation to her who had been an outsider, rejected by society; he drew her once more into the fellowship. In his encounter with doubting Thomas, Jesus transformed the hesitations and perplexities of the uncertain disciple so that his doubts became growing points in a developing faith. In Christ's contacts with a widening circle of friends after the resurrection, fresh hopes turned a bewildered and scattered group into a purposeful fellowship and a responsible community.

Christ's own prayers were offered for large issues. He prayed for unity and those prayers which are offered through him share his uniting love. He prayed for peace, not for a mere cessation of hostilities, but for a particular quality of peace, based on a forgiving love and a reconciliation of opposites. He upheld the sick and troubled with a prayer of abiding love, finding a spiritual disease behind the maladjustment of life and the conflict of persons. To pray by the power and might of Christ creates that trust and confidence we seek when 'alone with Him'.

Keeping In Touch

Points of contacts are elusive. We ask to be introduced at a party among strangers and hover uncertainly before the words come and the silence is broken. The only way to learn how to pray is to pray. To hear a greeting from a friend or a stranger is to have a chance to reply, to make a beginning, and to be in touch. Too often we fail to begin and are vexed that the spirit does not move us. The simple salutation 'The Lord be with you' stirs memories of spiritual happenings in both Old and New Testaments. If we hear it at public worship and join with others in responding 'and with thy spirit . . . and also with you', we can hear it also in the company of Christ. The God who is always more ready to hear than we are to pray is there first, if only we could listen and respond. He starts us praying. We only need to keep our appointment with him, and to be there.

We need more meeting points. They are precious occasions in our life together. Too much of human activity lacks coherence. We live and work in parallel lines. Spasmodic efforts of rather aimless fits and starts need to be disciplined and co-ordinated. 'The Lord be with you' when used as a greeting for one or a few or a large crowd is an invitation for all our talents to be drawn together and to be used to the best advantage under the guidance of the Spirit. The Spirit unifies and develops for purposes often only partially disclosed what each one of us has to offer. 'Be it unto me according to thy word' is far from representing a merely mechanical reflex or a feebly acquiescent reply. Its power as a response lies in the attitude of positive humility it indicates. We appreciate its readiness to allow a great thing to begin in a small way. If a slave prayed 'Christ be with me', he was already shedding his slave mentality. He was opting for a change of master.

A readiness to be committed and to give ourselves away is very different from being enslaved. Voluntary service may sound a contradiction in terms; yet it takes the place of drudgery and dullness. Grim compulsions become transformed into absorbing committal. Time flies in such a Lent.

Many Christians feel themselves to be prisoners of their own history and strive to find release. Lent is a time when, by seeking the presence of Christ, our prejudices can be examined and inhibitions faced. It is a time for casting care upon Him, for He cares for us. Life's priorities cry out to be sorted and re-arranged in the light of His life. It is not possible to re-write history: nor is it wise to forget it, since there are lessons to be learnt from our mistakes and the traditions, social and racial, which have moulded us. In the presence of Christ, it is a privilege and duty to be self-critical; confessing our sins and short-comings with a new-found freedom. To be with Him is to hear another side to the human story we tell about ourselves. Christ with us helps us to find our bearings and a new starting point.

'Where are you?'* is one of the first questions asked in the scriptures. It is a question to put to ourselves. It will form a healthy piece of self-examination. To be placed in the right relationship with Christ immediately involves our relationship with others.

It has been pointed out that the theme 'lost and found' can be traced like a thread running through the books of the Bible. There is a hiding from God and a seeking for him from beginning to end. As the scriptures tell of God's ways with us, so we read in succession a story of rescue and salvation. We need only to begin with the garden scene of Eden to capture the message. The man and the woman hid themselves from the presence of the Lord God among the trees and the Lord God said, 'Where are you?' Ever since there have been displaced persons, drop-outs, lost souls, disorientated men and women.

In the records of biblical history, a selfish, grasping king is rebuked and called to order by the prophet whose role it is to proclaim God's will and God's judgment; that prophet had the unpopular task of opening drains, figuratively speaking, and pointing at smells, such was the state of society around him. The king seeks to avoid a meeting and a clash with this

*Genesis 3, 9.

27

disturbing prophet, but he cannot escape. His conscience is caught and cornered. King Ahab cries out to the prophet Elijah, 'Have you found me, O my enemy?!'* All through history, God in the lives of his prophets, disciples, and other faithful adherents has sought out those who would escape and hide from life's realities, who shut their eyes to brothers' needs, who are blind at heart, who look the other way, and will not see.

Christ within me

At this point our prayers strikes to a deeper level. The thought contained in the phrase is a familiar one for those who hear in it the echo of such fervent spiritual discoveries as 'I am crucified with Christ; nevertheless I live; not I, but the Christ that lives in me'.

Christ comes first. Each repeated phrase of the Christ-filled stanza of the Breastplate brings us back to Him as the beginning and the initiator of all that we attempt. He dwells in us and we in Him; yet He does not overwhelm us or absorb us. He wants us to be ourselves. He longs to be in our hearts, within us. He was made man: He was thus totally involved in our conditions of living and in the limitations of our human affairs. Knowing what was in man, He desires us to be totally involved in His conditions, now that He is risen, ascended, and glorified. Here is identification; this is the inwardness of His life and ours, in the closest relationship.

Saint Patrick in all likelihood conformed when at home with his parents, and practised the religion of his Christian upbringing without openly rebelling. In his *Confession*, however, something rather different comes to the surface; he admitted that he 'forsook God and

*I Kings, 21, 20.

did not keep His commandments'. He was aware of his falling away from the faith, his apostasy and he expressed himself in very frank terms about his sceptical outlook. This inner feeling he put into words after he had left the sheltered protection of home. He saw himself more honestly with an independent eye and a measure of detachment, when out on his own without visible means of support. This self-awareness proved to be a turning point in his spiritual odyssey. He had discovered Christ and became convinced that he belonged to Him. The excitement of assimilating this experience gave him the courage to take the next step and to shake off the shackles that imprisoned his whole being. His ecstasy could well have been translated into a joyous shout of praise; 'My God and King! He lives in me and I in Him'.

Patrick spoke with a rugged honesty of his unworthiness. We read in the *Confession*, 'The Lord my God regarded my low estate and kept me before I knew Him'. Again, he wrote 'after I came to Ireland, the love of God and His fear came to me more and more, and my faith was strengthened, and my spirit was so moved that in a single day I would say as many as a hundred prayers'. The description of another spiritual experience startles us as we read 'that same night, when I was asleep, Satan assailed me violently, a thing I shall remember as long as I shall be in this body. And he fell upon me like a huge rock, and I could not stir a limb . . . and I believe that I was sustained by Christ my Lord and that His Spirit was even then crying out on my behalf, and I hope it will be so in the day of my tribulation, as it is written in the Gospel. On that day, the Lord declares, it is not you that speak but the Spirit of your Father that speaketh in you.

Christ within me. It is a prayer of contemplation. Nothing is fully known unless it is first contemplated. An old saying urges us to contemplate and then to pass on to others what we have contemplated. We take in what is given to us. We look to Jesus not simply as an example to follow nor yet as a forerunner who leads and inspires; rather we find in Him the one in whom we live and move and have our being. He forms our inner life. He is the constant companion who fills the Christian's life.

In this interior life, Patrick heard voices and saw visions. 'We ask thee, boy, come and walk among us once more', he seemed to hear. He was not the first to have received the invitation 'Come over and help us'. His words are deeply mystical in spite of the simple naïveté of his autobiography: 'another night—whether within me or beside me I know not, God knoweth—they called me unmistakably with words which I heard but could not understand, except that at the end of the prayer He spoke thus: "He that has laid down His life for thee, it is He that speaketh in thee"; and so I awoke full of joy. And again I saw him praying in me, and I was as it were within my body and I heard him above me, that is over the inward man, and there he prayed mightily with groanings'.

We perceive in this inner life, first the voice of vocation, and then the voice of conscience. The two lie close to one another in many a life.

Vocation comes clear when the urge from within prompts us to service. The signs of this may be both external and internal. A calling sounds in our ears at our prayers when the love of Christ constrains us and the goodness of God by its very attractiveness stirs a response from us. The power of the Spirit makes use of us in our weakness; the grace of God perfects our nature. We are summoned to serve; we are called out as members of one another to do His will. The Christian church consists of those who are called out. Long before Christ's coming, Moses, Isaiah, Jeremiah, among the outstanding figures in the drama of the history of the Old Testament, sensed that they were called. Although they were leaders, they were deeply conscious of their inadequacy, and yet they said 'yes' to the call that came to them. They responded to the compelling character of the invitation which was presented to them. The humble diffidence of Moses proved that his spiritual gifts could be made perfect, or fitted for the required end, in and through weakness. Jeremiah described himself as a child. Yet his vocation was to be one of special quality and maturity. He was one of those 'called upon to abandon the fixed orders of religion which the majority of the people still considered valid— a tremendous step for a man of the ancient east to take —and because of it the prophets, in their new and completely unprecedented situation, were faced with the need to justify themselves both in their own and in other people's eyes'*. Isaiah was smitten to the core by his own sinfulness; his encounter with God's holiness made the contrast between him and his maker agonizing indeed. His first reaction was: 'Woe is me. I am lost'. There he stood, however, and could do no other than utter 'here am I; send me'.

'Christ is within us as our Teacher', St. Augustine wrote to his pupils. 'If you cannot understand words falling from my lips but reaching only to your ears, turn to Him in your hearts who teaches me what to say

*G. von Rad, Old Testament Theology, quoted in E. W. Nicholson, commentary on Jeremiah, chapters 1–25. OUP, 1973. p. 24.

and gives to you such capacity as He deems fit . . . . He may defer giving but He will never allow the hungry to go away empty'. Today His voice can be heard.

Conscience is an inner awareness of God's love and God's nature. We use knowledge best, not through the study of separate subjects but by relating all things— the whole creation—to Him through whom and by whom are all things. Christ as the Lord of life is the co-ordinator. The knowledge of Christ is not specialised, yet it is based on facts of experience, supported by evidence, illuminating every human activity and interest. If Christ is within me, how can I fear anything outside me? How can I fear any more 'the enemy within' that has disturbed and unsettled me?

It is what comes from within and then finds outward expression in actions and attitudes that marks the man. The mind, if conscientious, makes moral judgments and ponders on rights and wrongs. The love that suffers long and is kind stands out as the most excellent of the spiritual gifts. We need the whole Christ in our lives to integrate us, to bring inner harmony, to mirror for us the extent of our human potential. Conscience is an awareness of the right judgment that we can make through the Spirit's power. If we ignore the love of Christ and display instead a callousness, a great refusal, and a spiritual emptiness, this sensitive knowledge will become dull and stunted; our inner life will ring hollow.

Patrick was sensitive, like others, when called to his ministry. One of the ways in which we can sharpen our awareness of need for guidance lies in an appreciation of God's goodness, a sense of wonder at the justice of His standards. So we set our pettiness beside His greatness, our shallowness beside the deep reserves of His power and compassion; our short-sighted, short-term efforts beside His patience and long-suffering. If we are betrayed by what is false within, we are also spurred on to attempt great things for God, yet not we ourselves, but the Christ who dwells in us, the Christ within.

Slow growth in the tender roots of the spirit we seldom tolerate. Yet, the firmest friendships, when spiritually grounded, are gradually, sensitively made, not in a day, nor in the course of a world cruise, but more probably in ordinary work-a-day surroundings where shared incentives bring fellowship and abiding love.

Side by side with slow growth we are only too conscious of wasted energy and superficial sprouting. Many a good word of advice and wisdom is welcomed, and then shrivels. Every sower reckons with wastage. Even in the action of the precision instruments of the seeder and fertiliser, mechanically propelled, there are losses to be cut; the tough climate takes its seasonal toll; the ravages of bird, beast, and insect defy the farmer's opposition. Spiritual life has its wastage too. Wandering thoughts, selfish desires, vague and woolly efforts must not discourage the servant of God from starting again and achieving something well-aimed and constructive, as he prays and plans for the future, refusing to panic.

As the seed grows secretly in the soil, so in God's underground hidden forces are rallying and gathering strength. Sometimes on the surface of the world's affairs, it seems as if no successful Christian action can be taken to bring peace to a community or to settle disputes in the international scene. The lesser of two evils seems to be the only choice in a dilemma; the perfect policy is impracticable. Only secretly, anonymously can the seed germinate on its way to further growth in order to produce fruitful results in the future.

Prayers of heart-broken mothers for their wayward sons and daughters appear to sound unheard; many hints are not taken; the force of example looks feeble. Yet it is not by dictation nor by arrogant compulsion that thoughts are sown for sound and proper rooting and fruiting. Through dark and discouraging days in the stretch of Lent we grope and stumble in the hope that inner forces are being rallied in preparation for some open action. The grace of God is the seed of any promised glory.

Chapter 3

Christ behind me, Christ before me

The spiritual journey continues. Faith has often been expressed in terms of bodily movement. 'Walking' rather than 'thinking' or 'believing' illustrates the meaning of practising the faith as a way of life. Moving on step by step, rather than shutting the eyes and holding the breath, indicated that faith increased when steps of faith were taken. Faith is one of the commodities that finds its store increasing the more it is consumed. It can never be wasted even when lavished on the most trivial detail of the day's programme. To live by faith is to find growing points of faith sprouting in every corner.

Faith has been defined as 'a God-placed trust'. In particular situations, it is seen as a gift. This gift needs placing. God places it in unexpected and unpromising surroundings at times. The gift also deserves a welcome and a reception. It is sometimes more blessed to receive than to give. The gracious receiver is an asset in any company. The soil in which faith is sown is the stuff of our energies, our growing, and our habits. Prayer also is concerned with the environment.

In all our lives there is a past and a future. The past

must be reckoned with, not swept under the carpet. Our history, whether in family or country, needs understanding. Our personal background, when studied and appreciated, helps to explain our outlook and accounts for many of our pre-suppositions, and our emotional reactions. There is much that we have inherited. We note tendencies in ourselves that bear an undisputed family likeness. Those of us, who love our homes and the atmosphere of local beauty spots we have known from childhood, will know the existence and strong influence of our traditions. We perceive the advantages and disadvantages of lives that are set in the mid-stream of history. There are obvious limitations surrounding lives that are never starkly independent and certainly cannot be self-sufficient. It is natural for some to cut away from a limiting environment and seek a fresh start. In spiritual terms we find within the framework of what has been given us in life wonderful scope for spontaneity and precious human freedoms.

Prayer provides an example of spontaneous loving action made possible within the very limits that might seem to stifle and frustrate. Someone has said that the past, which so dogs us that we feel it hanging over our heads like a curse, needs to be remembered in order to be forgotten. Paul Tillich has pointed out that this is a way of defining forgiveness. It provides the antidote to the sweeping of troubles and faults out of sight in the hope that they will go away or at least be forgotten.

The pilgrim discovers his journey to be a kind of exodus—a journey out. The well-known exodus from Egypt across the Red Sea under the leadership of Moses and Aaron was both physical and spiritual, an experience and a release, a testing and an ordeal. 'The Lord went before them by day in a pillar of cloud, to lead them along the way, and by night in a pillar of fire'.* The journey was extensive geographically and dangerous historically, but spiritually and theologically, it was redemptive. A going forth in obedience to a definite lead and a clear command was part of the history of God's people. The Christian to-day has a history behind him to encourage as well as to warn him. The story of the journey of the children of Israel was not only a matter of chronicling their history; the main facts of the saga were woven into their worship, their life and culture. The Psalms sing of the journey, recounting what was behind and before them, in verse and in paeans of thanksgiving; the full history was imprinted on their memories and each generation learned the facts by heart. Exodus became a way of life. All life was a moving out from the darkness of the strange land, from the slavery of a dread captivity, through difficult conditions by sea and in the desert, through long and dreary testing times of disheartenment, their faith often failing, and their trust eroded, with no food or drink to relieve the pangs of hunger and enforced fasting.

It was a journey of a life-time, a journey to be remembered. The turning of the narrative into a psalm of praise was not intended to encourage a living in the past or to foster a morbid harking back leading to self-pity and frustration. Rather the events of the journey were in themselves causes of thanksgiving. They increased a people's reverence for God who had piloted them through the difficulties and rescued them from the dangers. 'This God is our God for ever and ever: He shall be our guide until death'.† This was the burden of

*Exodus 13, 21.
†Psalm 48,13.

37

their song of praise.

The promise was always before them, no matter how grim the experiences behind. A bare existence, under tyrannical domination, with no life they could call their own, was to be transformed into a life in a land promised to them where they would have a home after exile and a portion of land for themselves and their families. Here would be found an opportunity to increase and to flourish and to find that fulfilment, sometimes called 'peace'. This genuine peace, if the word 'shalom' can convey its rich meaning to us, must be explained as wholeness, healing, and all that is meant by physical and spiritual health and happiness.

In our study of journeys we find that those on the way and on the move discover not only places but themselves and their own place in life. They see not only the passing sights; they gain insight, as they encounter changes of customs and climate, new experiences in other places, among other peoples.

Jesus on his journey up to Jerusalem turns the travel and the route into a course of training and teaching for those who accompany him on the way. As they went along with him they discovered that He himself was the Way. The faith He taught was soon to be called the Way. The message of the Kingdom which He proclaimed was applied with great definiteness to the people He met, in whose particular lives He became personally involved.

'*Christ behind me, Christ before me*' may be a thousand-year-old prayer but it is without doubt in tune with what we hear from missionaries and explorers on their wanderings and expeditions. Patrick's journey is a vivid pilgrim's progress; the loneliness far away from home and the hopeful expectations of a voyage out from the shores of the island test his faith. Likewise Columba's sailing after exile from Ireland became a blessing and no disgrace; his new beginning closely linked with lessons from the past were built upon penitence and hope.

Christian thanksgiving is measured by milestones on the road we journey. Such stages are marked by anniversaries, days of commemoration that tell of our indebtedness to many known and unknown helpers and friends from the past. The words of Edward Reynolds' prayer of General Thanksgiving remind us that, however evil the days, there are always grounds for gratitude. We praise God for 'our creation, preservation and all the blessings of this life'. There is evidence that the author of these lapidary phrases was speaking from the heart and incidentally was suffering at the same time from an illness which in his day, three centuries ago, was pronounced incurable. We thank God primarily, however, not for what he has done but for what he is. We are surrounded by God: He is behind and before. Brendan the Navigator was surrounded by the wide, wide sea in his small craft and gained a special sense of God's mercy. The Breton prayer strikes a similar note 'O my God, have pity on me; thy sea is so large, my boat is so small'. The moving words of Psalm 139 cannot have been far from the thoughts of our Christ-centred prayer 'thou hast beset me behind and before and laid thine hand upon me'.

Sometimes we want to be not where we are with many responsibilities pressing on us, but elsewhere. We are not thankful enough for our present lot and positioning, because we failed to notice what we have been given and what we have inherited from those who have preceded us. Those who learn their history—and geography—from researches and observations of their own, find hidden goods in very ordinary surroundings. They are astounded as they work on their project to discover what has been there all the time unappreciated, not even noticed. They dig up the past and find fascinating surprises in antiquities and archaeological discoveries; in so doing they also gain a clearer understanding of the present. They are able to trace life's developments; they learn from the experiments and mistakes of those who have foraged for the truth and probed into the causes of things. Many have stumbled on the right answers or else have failed to perceive their way through a mist and a wilderness.

The Way Ahead

There is a world of difference between a problem and a mystery in a life of uncertainties and difficulties. We may not know what is before us on a journey. We move on in faith. Some difficulties and problems are too baffling for us to face, we say. We do not know where to begin. We hover on the edge and cannot find a clue or make a beginning.

The Christian has failed to find the answer to many questions asked by those who have great faith. It is the same with those who have little or no faith. The candid Christian knows that much has been unanswered in the problems of suffering, death, eternal life and the unknown future. Yet the approach to the questions posed about these subjects is of the highest importance. The Christian is on the right track if he does not treat these matters simply as human problems, as subjects to be left with philosophers, scientists, and even the theologians. Every Christian can enter into the themes in the spirit of research. Each one of us is called upon to struggle with life; many have to endure pain; all should prepare for death. In the process of such exploring, much is discovered and the findings can in a limited way be passed on. These things are mysteries rather than problems.

We are right to allow ourselves to be wrapped round by the dazzling darkness of these and other mysteries. It is not unlike entering a dimly lighted room and depending on our ability to grope for some recognisable piece of furniture to help us to find our bearings. Some are quick in those unfavourable conditions to catch a glimpse and a gleam of a clue. We plunge into the middle of things in our lives and often know little of the behind and before. We need to understand the context of to-day's events, but as often as not we are swept into the 'to-day' and may either be sharing an experience with many others or else undergoing a pain or a pleasure which cannot be communicated; much less can it be understood.

There is much in our findings that cannot be passed on to others. We are only able to describe what we have seen and heard by comparisons. An illustration provides a comparison but cannot convey all that we have felt and gained from what we have been through. The simple example of the tooth-ache, that sends sharp agony through our being, demonstrates the personal commitment and responsibility that fall upon us as individual persons, as unique personalities. The other pains of the spirit: loneliness, the lost feeling, the sense of being deserted and of no one caring, and the chill of despair are all current happenings in many lives; they may be alleviated by the knowledge that others are in a far worse state, by the example of those who have triumphed over adversity, but they can never be fully shared or paralleled. For such hazards on the journey, the Christian style of life is shaped by the spirit in which we can move through life's mysteries influenced by what God has to give us in such situations. The approach, the attitude, the mood claim our attention as we try to go through the present predicament and do not seek to side-step or escape it.

In our study of the Bible, we learn about the 'behind and before'. St. Paul's letter to the Roman refers to 'the whole creation groaning and travailing' and ourselves 'groaning within ourselves . . . waiting . . .'. The same letter devotes the eleventh chapter to a potted history of God's dealing 'in times past' with his people; this is not mere antiquity, past and over; it serves as a living interpretation of what life is like. The eleventh chapter on faith in the letter to the Hebrews provides not a long and tedious list of names but a line of life, a thrilling picture of God's consistent and continuous action, through the lives of men and women who 'attempted great things for God' and 'expected great things' from Him.

We might describe this account of faith's journey and progress as a kind of roll of honour. Indeed it is often read by Christians at the end of their year of worship as a reminder of what God has done through people and why.

The list is not exhaustive; it could scarcely be so. Time would fail and space would not permit anyone to tell the full story of those who 'through faith conquered kingdoms, enforced justice, received promises, and stopped the mouths of lions'. Many besides the heroes mentioned in the catalogue of the letter to the Hebrews showed in their lives or by their deeds that 'faith is the assurance of things hoped for, the conviction of things not seen' or, in other words, that 'faith gives substance to our hopes, and makes us certain of realities we do not see'.*

One of the fascinating features of Christian life is that the fruit of heroism is not mass-produced. Each life reveals something fresh about the power of the spirit to bring the best and the unexpected from the characters of those who live by faith. There have been mass conversions to Christianity as we learn from recent missionary history, but each life in the crowd has the opportunity of expressing individually and uniquely a truth about Jesus Christ.

The faith of Noah appears in the list; it is sharply contrasted with the faith of Abraham. The lives of these two differed in circumstances and orientation. Noah's faith was shut-in; Abraham's ventured forth. Noah's faith served as a fortress against the foe outside. His ark became a spiritual centre, where the few, rescued from the flood's destruction, kept alive the invisible goods of trust and truth by withdrawing from the danger and protecting what had been committed to them. The ark in later days symbolised the church that preserved life and fostered spiritual survival. Through his faith, Noah 'put the whole world in the wrong and made good his own claim to the righteousness which comes of faith'. Such faith nourished an other-worldliness rather than an unworldliness in the hearts of the ark's crew. Faith in our day must be given conditions of growth in the worship of churches, in the peace and quiet of private life, in a certain detachment from life through self-denial and abstinence. This is, however, only a part of faith's functions and activities.

A different and complementary emphasis in the

*Hebrews, 11, 1.

practice of faith was illustrated by Abraham. He reached out to a new country, to other people and places, to an apparently limitless horizon. Rather than concentrating in one area and bearing his witness in strict apartness, he went out adventurously, not knowing where he was going to. Step by step he sought a city whose builder and maker was God. He acted with a hopefulness and an optimism in many unpromising situations. This proved the reality of his faith as a principle of living. He left his home, he became a stranger, he started a family, he made sacrifices, all through his journeyings he became conscious of his destiny and the ultimate worth of his endeavours.

Inward and out-going faith, such as these two heroes typified, are needed in the lives of us and our contemporaries. In this way history is made and tradition shaped. The roll of honour tells us less of the meaning of faith in the abstract than of the results that faith produces in the lives of individuals and the stories of nations.

We read of the past not to live in the past but to trace how promises issued in fulfilment and also to learn about the providence of God. The Bible is a library of books about God who was revealed in history and who was known in and through the doings of good and evil people; He was seen to be a power as well in tragedies as in triumphs. A history of salvation is traced through the lives of the people of the Book.

Christ entered this history. The 'behind' was to be termed B.C. and the 'before' became A.D. The era of Christianity or the age of faith is the context of our lives. We are in it; we are committed to it. So we date the Christ event and recall that his ministry began when Pontius Pilate was governor. This unique event of the birth of Christ and his life in the world was steeped in history, rooted in a particular soil, expressed in terms of a culture.

We study the Bible in order that we may understand more fully what took place under God. We are his people, too. We seek to claim the family portraits, as someone said, when we identify ourselves with the people of the book. We find Abraham's life illuminating as we study the meaning of membership in church, family, and community. His faith in responding to a call and moving out trustfully is the kind of faith that summons us. We admire his certain faith in the apparently uncertain future.

We sing the psalms and make them our songs of praise, celebrations of our deliverances from sins and sorrows. Our feelings and spiritual discoveries are often summed up precisely and completely in phrases and felicitous quotations from the songbook of Israel. We, too, ask God to preserve our going out and our coming in. We are aware that God has searched us out and known us . . . that such knowledge is too wonderful and excellent for us, we cannot attain unto it.

The claiming of the prophets as teachers who speak for us, as interpreters of the times in which we live is part of our Christian programme of action and education. They reproved, rebuked, exhorted and advised as did Paul the apostle of the Gentiles in his New Testament letters. The word they spoke for their day is a word of wisdom and truth for us, since human needs have altered little basically, and the timeless, undated fruits of faith, hope and love are the things which we must live for.

Questions are often asked about the 'before'. What for example about the prophecies of doomsday, the world's end and the collapse of civilisation as we know it? What has been the use of all the years of faith and what the meaning of the past and the purpose of God's revelation? It is not always easy to perceive that even if the end of all things came tomorrow, the good of all the past years would still be good. The witness of the faithful, the valiant and the true will not automatically be wasted or invalidated in the face of catastrophe. Such is the mystery of time as well as of eternity.

Contemplation of the 'behind and before' encourages us to examine the relationship of time to the timeless. We are able to gain a sense of perspective as we discern the significance of the crisis, the hour, the era, the moment of truth. 'Christ and time' is the title of a book which helps to distinguish for us the spirit of the age from the age of the spirit. Prayer, for example, is a means of linking a moment of time with timelessness, eternity and God's presence; it lifts us out of this world and yet adds to our life in this world a dimension at once inspiring and fulfilling.

The Lord's Prayer, like the Christ who taught it, is the same yesterday, to-day, and for ever. It has been translated into many languages; many more versions of it exist than can fit on the panels of the Pater Noster church outside Jerusalem on the hill of the Ascension. It has, however, a single message for a multiplicity of peoples and countries, races and cultures. Daily bread, as essential sustenance for the body, is a shared need. Daily acknowledgment of our dependence upon God for all life's needs is never superfluous.

We remember the past but not in its entirety. We can

be too choosy, forgetting the uncomfortable, viewing the scene with one eye closed, losing perspective, relying on the half-truths, presented with bias or inaccurately reported. If any past event is linked by prayer to the God who is the Lord of history we will be more likely to learn with balance and fairness the full lessons of the past. Such a wide and generous vision as the Creator of the world provides will shield us from over-simplifications, narrowness of mind, provincialism in outlook and much selfish pride and prejudice.

There is an omnipresence in this 'behind and before'. God bridges time. No limits are set to his power. Nothing human is outside his concern or beyond his care. Christ leads us through no darker rooms than he went through before. The nine day's wonder fades rapidly into the background of oblivion; to-day's headline news is the banner of the moment to be replaced by the next sensation, novelty or peculiarity. The word of the Lord endures, on the other hand, for ever. The startling event must be read and noticed; it is news and ought not to be suppressed. But it needs a context, and requires a reader with a sense of proportion, with critical faculties trained and alert, with an awareness of the 'behind and before'.

The famous prayer that asks God to grant that as we pass through things temporal we may finally lose not the things eternal, comes to life as the days pass. The course of history reveals life's constants and the repetition of many of those constants in the changing patterns. Everything in human experience tapers off into mystery.

The people from the past whom we remember with gratitude for what they were and gave to the world help us to increase our thankfulness to God. Many types have illustrated the richness and variety of life. They have not all been saints but the force of their example has been eloquent and effective. Lessons from the past have included protests and failures. There have been voices crying in the wilderness, unheeded in their day, but later seen to be wise and true in the days in which their works followed them.

Chapter 4

Christ beside me

The prayer throws light on the power and place of intercession. The word has many shades of meaning. One interpretation is a delicate one; 'falling in beside another' describes co-operation and a relationship, not in the least aggressive, yet showing a willingness to be committed. The interceder, at this point of contact or association, is not only beside the one for whom he is concerned, but also on his side. The metaphor may be from drill; the interceder lines up in order to form part of the movement or operation. There is togetherness here. It is not a question of an interceder praying for another individual on a private basis; of two trying to walk together on difficult ground, yet agreeing. The intent and action are wider than this. The interceder is part of a movement, a corporate action and, although his part may be a small one, and his contribution might scarcely be missed, if not forthcoming, yet it is significant, since it is personal, an expression of out-going love. What God may do with the team is not for a single member to estimate. The filling up of the gap, left in the twelve by the defection of Judas, was counted important; yet there is but a scant description of the abilities possessed by Matthias, the successful candidate in the by-election. As a witness with something to say with conviction about what he had seen and heard of Christ's resurrection, he possessed the vital qualification. He had also companied with the eleven colleagues all the time that the Lord Jesus went in and out among them. Christ had been beside him.

Intercessors are both with Christ and also with those in need of spiritual support and the reinforcement of corporate prayer. They line up. They bring themselves, their faith, their hope, their love into a situation where these powerful forces must be given opportunity. The distinctive prayers of the Christian are offered through Jesus Christ, with constant reference to Him, with His name lending credibility, and His character giving validity to all that we ask or think.

The intercessor falls in alongside Christ and alongside those that are Christ's. Christ's own intercession demands our study and our imitation. He prayed for sinners, for his enemies, for those who let him down in betrayal or through denial, for those who did not know what they were doing, although the deed to an outsider was repulsive and unutterably cruel. We conclude from this short list that nothing was past praying for. On the Cross, when physically powerless and reduced to humiliating defeat, his prayers continued. He prayed, so it seemed, without ceasing.

He prayed also for those who were with Him and not against Him. He did not overlook the fact that this kind of understanding, sympathetic prayer is needed even when there is no crisis, no calamity, no desperation. Where there is life, prayer is essential for direction, sustenance, growth, and progress. Christ prayed for his disciples, those that companied with Him; He prayed for their unity, their personal holiness, and their witness to the truth.

The seventeenth chapter of St. John's gospel contains the prayer of Christ at our side. 'One in Christ' is the scene pictured there, even when there are overtones of divisions and fragmentations, of tensions and intolerances, of bitternesses and bigotries.

Intercession is also a falling in beside others. Others may include those like us, related to us, of similar outlook and traditions; others must also include those different from us, those from whom we can learn, those whose co-operation we cannot dispense with, those whom we need to love—even if from the first we do not like them—because Christ is beside them, too, and Christ loves them.

Divisions among Christians cannot be healed without prayer. We know this in theory; it is the practice which we find difficult. The prayers for peace across the denominations in our country owe much to the special days appointed. Voices of scepticism have admittedly been raised to call such efforts in question as stunts or cries of despair from a last ditch. Prayers in the open air, in the market-place, across parish boundaries and congregational groupings have a quality all their own. A crowd is transformed into a community, a group into a fellowship, a casual gathering into a meeting with a purpose. Who stood beside us in the open air, when it rained and we sang hymns and made our response to the intercessions? I met a family of four several years after such a moment of open prayer, a hundred miles away from the place of intercession and heard their greeting with surprise as they addressed me and said 'we know you; we stood beside you at the prayers in the market square'. A trivial encounter, a passing acquaintanceship, or perhaps something more? If the members who meet in the name of Christ, who is present among the two or three, also pray for those beside them and join spiritual forces with them, then the meaning of 'the beloved community' springs to life and the barriers which hinder many from coming alongside each other begin to come down. The prayer at barricades, the existence of a peace line at the intersection of city streets in time of riot underline with a special poignancy the reality of the 'one in Christ', still a mighty potential.

Intercession has a dynamic meaning of a more thrustful kind. 'Moving in among people with concern for them' is an explanation of the exercise which helps us to understand the scope and influence of this kind of prayer. If the Greek word tells us where we are as interceders and points to our place and rôle, the Latin word indicates the practice, the activity, the co-operative movement which is intercession. The closing chapter of St. Paul's letter to the Romans is crammed with names, listed for greetings and prayers. The end of a mighty treatise on God's righteousness becomes unexpectedly personal. Names known and even unknown to the writer become important in this context, for they are the names of those for whom Christ died. No one is undeserving of mention; certainly no one is past praying for. The doctrine of God revealed in Jesus Christ is dynamic in as much as it compels this love and justice, this care and sacrifice to be extended to those who are God's and Christ's. It is not surprising that theory and practice are thus held together; there is the same partnership between doctrine and life. Prayer moves in among people of every nation and tongue. 'Intercession is a social act'.

Prayer is a moral movement. When we pray, we are right to make large petitions which set our requests in a wide perspective, with sights set high. We pray for lasting and serviceable gifts that we wish others to have; we present to God root-needs and the priorities as we see them. 'Pray that my faith may not fail', said the air-pilot to his mother in war-time, as he prepared to take off on a perilous patrol, 'do not concentrate on my personal safety. I really want the courage, nerve and spirit to carry out my duty. I want strength to do the difficult things given to me to undertake. I do not want to escape from my obligations'. The mother had been praying that at the last minute the flight might be called off.

The movement of intercession requires directing and marshalling. There are great possibilities here. The power available could easily be dissipated and become less effective, if in disarray. 'Christ beside me' reminds us of Christian prayer offered 'through Jesus Christ our Lord'. The things we ask for must be alike in character and shape to the requests made by Jesus when he prayed for his people.

Early Christian prayers such as 'Brethren, pray for us' would be found scratched on a wall, perhaps with a simple cross carved beside it, to symbolise the complete and final sign of conquering love. The Chi Rho of early times and the letters IHS, a shortened form of the name of Jesus, showed how the name conveyed the living personality, the character, and the saving work of Christ. Ultimately we pray for people because Christ died for them. If we consistently recall this, we will cease to be rigidly selective or sectional or unduly clannish, however natural it may be to have favourites. We are right to pray that 'we and all thy whole Church may obtain remission of our sins and all other benefits of his passion'.

Christian Caring

We sometimes ask if it is not patronising or condescending of us to pray for others when we ourselves are so full of faults and in sore need of prayer. The question is raised in different forms. The activity of intercession prompts such queries as: 'what have we to bring? How can we help in this way? What difference can we make to this or that crisis?' Such question marks are readily understood. Yet we need to consider a wider and a deeper approach. We pray with people rather than for them.

The word 'condescend' as used in the New Testament is worth examining. Needless to say it bears a different meaning from the current and common interpretation. It also helps to answer our doubts about presumptuousness in praying with and beside others. The following famous list of directions for the Christian brings us to the crucial word; 'rejoicing in hope, patient in tribulation, continuing instant in prayer; distributing to the necessity of saints—given to hospitality. Bless them which persecute you, bless, and curse not. Rejoice with them that do rejoice, and weep with them that weep. Be of the same mind one to another. Mind not high things, but *condescend* to men of low estate'.* Only at the end of the list do we appear to find a touch of paternalism that seems to spoil the spontaneity of this magnificent range of Christian action and to blight the humility that loves people effortlessly for their own sake, just because they are people.

The modern translations of the Bible clearly resent

*Romans 12, 12–16.

the uppish sound of this word 'condescend'. The Jerusalem Bible goes so far as to translate 'Mind not high things, but condescend to men of low estate' by a bold stroke of ingenious interpretation with the words 'never be condescending, but make real friends with the poor'. We may well wonder how an end has been made to condescension in this way. The original word however is one of those 'fellowship' words used by St. Paul who pictured Christian service as essentially a combined operation, something done by the faithful together, corporately. The word translated 'condescend' had not the meaning of 'looking down the nose' or 'stooping from some lofty pedestal'; it could bear the interpretation, in the popular language of the papyrus writing of the time, 'to be be led away with others to execution or prison'. Thus the writer might be understood as exhorting his readers to share prison with those in this wretched plight. Indeed, 'visiting prisoners' was one of the acid tests outlined by our Lord in the scene of the great assize: 'I was in prison and ye came (not) unto me'.* Condescend therefore in this bible passage need mislead us no longer. There is nothing basically snobbish or lofty in the word which points at any so-called superiorities in rank or class. It is a word that encourages voluntary, sacrificial and generous service given to others for the sake of the brotherhood and fellowship that we all enjoy in Christ. The Christian is urged to sit where prisoners and debtors sit; he identifies himself with the whole community in its troubles. There is self-denial, but no self-satisfaction here; there is humility, not superiority; there is the readiness to share with the true sympathy that suffers; there is no detached bestowing of largess. Christ's descent into the presence of the

*Matthew 25, 36.

55

departed and his traditional ministration to the spirits in prison was condescension with a difference. Out of the deep of death and suffering, Christian action triumphs more than we know. Like many words, condescension needs re-minting in our day. If love is taken into deep places of pain and desolation, there will follow upon the downward movement an ascent into a life made new and glorious. In prayer as in other human action there is such a thing as stooping to conquer.

Dietrich Bonhoeffer thinks aloud about his frustrations and from his own imprisonment helps us through similar experiences

"I'm afraid I'm bad at comforting. I can listen all right, but I can hardly ever find anything to say. But perhaps the way one asks about some things and not about others helps to suggest what really matters; and it seems to be more important actually to share someone's distress than to use smooth words about it. I've no sympathy with some wrongheaded attempts to explain away distress . . . so I don't try to explain it. I sometimes think that real comfort must break in just as unexpectedly as the distress."

In intercession we are not required to particularise. We need not say anything; we are probably on the wrong lines if we specify detailed answers and forecast results. We bring people and we bear in mind their plight in a trustful spirit, leaving them and ourselves there in touch. This kind of support given by intercession has been valued all through the centuries. The interceder himself felt supported in his own task; the one whom he remembers in prayer has been strengthened by such fellowship.

The popularity of 'vigils' has provided an example of the stimulus given to a community by meeting in the darkness of the night and watching in silence, waiting on God until the streaks of the dawn light appear for a new day and a fresh beginning. Music without words as well as words said or sung together punctuating the silence can express the response and longings of those who are 'with one mind in one place'. Here prejudices fall away; inhibitions no longer stifle; the Spirit moves to stir and to fire those who have up to this point found little meaning or relevance in worship and prayer.

A memorable vigil held in the city at a time of riot and violence was organised under the name of 'Shalom again'. It was a repeat effort. Many of the participants had watched together at an earlier date in the name of 'Shalom', the Hebrew word for 'peace with a distinctive slant'. Shalom can mean fulfilment, a perfecting of life so that it may be lived in the wholeness of dedication, fair dealing, true happiness which come from serving God and fellow human beings. In an earlier watch, Michel Quoist had come among this fellowship of youth to speak out of his life and work, marked also by conflicts and troubles. His prayers, his conversations and the answering of the questions that followed concentrated upon the 'building up of human life', as he phrased it.

In the patience of the vigil, in the testing time of watching for a few hours, many were stabbed awake to an appreciation of life's meaning and life's possibilities. Penitence, renewal, fresh insights and clearer thinking were found by those who watched and listened. Experience of this gift of peace, called shalom, has to be sought again and again. Prayers of life during the troubled hours in the suffering city made that vigil for the whole company a night to remember.

Much of the ordering of intercession must be left to each individual. There is value in corporate intercession at certain hours arranged beforehand and on specific days. The silent minute observed for world peace; the mid-day prayer for those in the midst of the whirl of business and commerce; the apportioning of certain subjects for particular days of the week; the observance of the year's seasons for remembrances and thanksgiving, all help to give balance and a generous comprehensiveness to an activity which by definition should never grind to a halt but rather be marked by a continuous onward flow.

Midday Worship

A pattern of noon-day prayer is used on the American continent, counted suitable in the open prairies and also in the heat and humidity of the inner city. There is biblical evidence that the sickness of noon-day under a hot sun makes its impact upon the soul and spirit of man to depress him and even to make his prayers weary and worn. Prayers at noon are designed to recreate his spirit in the midst of his labours. These are short sharp 'arrow' petitions which relate work with worship both in the office and in the wide open spaces.

The mid-day prayers include the Lord's own prayer without which any order of prayer is the poorer: the phrases in it take fresh meaning from the context of coffee break or a breather amid the pressures of business. Then follow three pithily phrased prayers which pin-point noon-day moments in the life of Christ and some of his apostles. These prayers help to rescue time for spiritual renewal from the crowded hours that spell money and organisation in a world of packed schedules. They break into a tired, pressurised life with some time-less thoughts to put the day's doings in true perspective. We can learn through this kind of informal exercise in mid-day worship to consecrate two or at the most three minutes to God, asking Him to assist our spirits to grow, coming to a meeting place of deeper understanding in our faith.

It is not surprising that the first of the prayers following the 'Our Father' should recall the hour of agony upon the Cross at which our Lord achieved through suffering his mighty work of reconciliation. When the sun is high in the heavens, as it were, in full view of the horizons, we think upon 'the light of the world' whose way of light in the midst of darkness was the way of the cross. At mid-day we centralise this strange message of love which emerges from conflict and frustration in the doings of men.

It was at noon also that St. Paul saw a great light on the Damascus Road, a light which blinded him and blotted out a rebellious past. This incident flashed a vision upon an active, able life and sent it forward with a changed purpose in the same direction. Such a turning point, before the sun declines, stirs us to live in the present with a sense of responsibility and bids us refer all our abilities and skills to God for His controlling.

Saint Peter, too, had a mid-day moment. At the sixth hour, it is recorded, he went up to the house-top to pray: here his vision was renewed and enlarged. He saw his work, packed into a crowded life, as world work and himself as servant of the Spirit and not the master of things. The prayer woven round his experience of reaffirmed love and loyalty after denial and agnosticism tells us that prayers before lunch are not reserved for the enclosed monastic. There is a place for silence and recollection in the market and at the counter. An escape to the roof for peace and air has no slow-going implications. It may provide the opportunity for a cool decision, for recalling the quality and purpose of the end-product in manufacture or business to those who are still on the line. Prayers at noon bring our believing and caring into the centre of our day.

The world's great intercessors provide us with model prayers for us to use as we try to spread the movement. Published books of prayers contain a chain of prayer across the ages and also a life-line across the world. Many practical works of healing and philanthropy, enterprises of charity and human concern, have been, as one phrase puts it, 'cradled in prayer'. I recall the feeling of shame and inadequacy that came over me when on a journey abroad to visit a series of centres of Christian missionary life and work. Over and over again the workers amid all the strain and difficulty they faced with never-ending problems to tackle, with remedies always in short supply, emphasised the gratitude they felt for the never-failing support they received from the prayers of those of us at home. The realisation that the importance of this chain of prayer is not grasped and the vision of the far-distant work carried out by members of the family of God is a bleak and stunted one from our end increased the sense of urgency to repent of our neglect and luke-warm interest and to start afresh with more imagination and fuller information about these essential services of compassion and charity.

Information leaflets that supply facts and figures from the many countries where there is a Christian presence help to sustain the life of intercession. To be briefed with up-to-date news of progress and developments, to be aware of the new names of workers and leaders succeeding the old, will deepen interest and sympathy. All these ingredients help to make a prayer into a channel of love and concern. Those of us who admit to failure as interceders confess that their prayers have lapsed; but the very penitence about such apathy marks a readiness to start afresh. A moving prayer from an intercession of the Eastern Church puts the point 'those whom we have forgotten, do thou, O Lord, remember'. Those, on the contrary, who have nobly and faithfully kept in touch with the lonely pioneer and the isolated Christian in largely non-Christian surroundings have discovered that their memory for names and places has been kept alive and green; their zest for news does not flag: their function and devotion as communicators grows daily more effective.

Chapter 5

Christ to win me, Christ to comfort and restore me

The Breastplate was a protection. The weapons in 'the whole armour of God' described in the sixth chapter of St. Paul's letter to the Ephesians are the effective ones in the struggles which we face. In the use of them we will win through. An earlier verse of the Patrician hymn indicates the spirit of all we attempt and points to the ground of our confidence.

> 'I bind unto myself to-day
> The power of God to hold and lead;
> His eye to watch, His might to stay;
> His ear to hearken to my need.
> The wisdom of my God to teach;
> His hand to guide, His shield to ward;
> The word of God to give me speech;
> His heavenly host to be my guard'.

We are often left to discover that in wars and conflicts there are no victories. There may be a conclusion of hostilities and a cessation of strife, but exhaustion and suffering tend to eclipse the gains and blur the early issues. It is evident that when peace does come after war, a heavy responsibility for winning that peace is laid upon all.

All victories belong to God and His Christ. He overcomes evil with good. Those who seek settlements and happy relationships among churches, between sections of the community and political groupings must seek for the triumph of Christ over all the differences and points of contention. The individual Christian is called upon to surrender, to give up many things, and to deny himself. In this costing manner the way lies open for Christ to win him.

If we wish to win a race, we must keep in training. If we want to gain one thing above all others, we have to abandon the pursuit of many other things and deprive our lives of still more things, in spite of their attractiveness. This is the known practice for the athlete and the specialist in other fields; there is nothing distinctively Christian about such a problem of choice that faces everyone.

There are many things we humanly want and look for. It may be a safe job, or a prolonged holiday, or a little peace, or a comfortable fortune to be left to us. If we gain one wish, some other attraction tends to loom before us. There may be no end to our desires. Our small achievements on the school playing-fields fade into insignificance before dazzling successes in the market-places of the world. Yet even then we begin to want other things; we seek fresh conquests. There is in most of us a mixed feeling of anxiety and optimism about the view round the next corner. The anxiety springs from a lack of satisfying purpose which we sometimes dare to dignify with the title of 'divine discontent'. The optimism is reserved for a future still unknown. For in our craving for a multiplicity of things, we are fascinated, allured, and seduced, but never satisfied.

At first such toying with indecision carries with it an air of freedom. The dilettante soon finds himself not in paradise but in a wilderness. He begins to envy secretly the dull, unimaginative man of strong will and narrow vision, who at least knows what he wants and plods on persistently to his goal. His dogged temperament and iron discipline will have saved him from dissipating his energies and cluttering his life with futile irrelevancies. Yet he may leave a trail of destruction as he impoverishes his character and debases the humanness of his personality in his pursuit after speedy and tangible results.

The Christian at his best seeks a middle way between amiable, airy wanderings down the by-paths of passing fancy and the stern high-road that leads to crude success. Faced with many choices, the Christian desires one thing supremely. He does not aim at singleness of purpose in his search for a unified life, free from confusion and worry. He desires, in a picturesque phrase, 'the fair beauty of the Lord',* and expresses that desire through the worship of the holiest and a love for the highest. In this way, he finds that a great many things, unasked for and unspecified, are added to his life. The end he holds in view is completely satisfying. Inspired by Him who makes all things one, the Christian disciple finds that there is nothing greater or worthier for him to desire than God Himself.

What should we want most? Where are our priorities? We ask ourselves. The answer comes: we must want God. We seek first the kingdom of God. We ourselves stand in the way of this desire. We see the distinc-

*Psalm 27, 4.

64

tion between what might be called an accidental religion and a burning faith. Those who are accidentally religious fail to recognise the treasures of their goodly heritage. Most estimable people they often are who stem from a fine tradition but lack all conviction. They need to believe that there is something that prayer alone can supply. Awareness of the need of this sharing of God's life through prayer must be stirred in them before they are likely to gain anything from the observation of the conventions of organised religion. From the east comes a story to bear this out. An Indian boy came to his master and said to him 'I want God'. 'How much do you want him?' was the reply. 'O, I want God very much indeed'. 'Go', said the teacher, 'and put your head in that bowl of water over there and keep it there till I give you the sign'. The boy did as he was told and when eventually he received the sign, he was panting and spluttering for breath. 'Now, do you want God as much as that'? came the teacher's question. So we have to discover if belief is real; if it is a living belief, we will be ready to act on it, to do something about it. Herein lies the difference between an inherited belief and a belief of our own, a first hand conviction.

Jesus clearly loved the life around Him. He delighted in the company of children and enjoyed their play. His teaching is filled with illustrations from the beauty of nature and the enjoyment of growing things. He brings the birds and the flowers into His conversations about life and its possibilities. Many of His prayers are joyful expressions of thanksgiving. His approach to life and its opportunities is as positive as are His parables. Yet a shadow falls over His life and His message before very long. He said that a cross must be taken up by those following Him; not once or occasionally but daily. Life, if it is really to be abundant and victorious, must be lost before it can be gained.

It is more important to deny ourselves than to deny certain things to ourselves. The self has to be denied in Lent—and after. Egoism is out. Pure moralism and rigid rectitude will hardly achieve the abundant, victorious life; we may be left more self-centred than ever. In the presence of the Christ that wins us, prayer that stirs in us both repentance and renewal will rescue us from such self-centredness.

Christ won people by giving them his whole and undivided attention. He would concentrate on one single person in a crowd of a thousand. He would look on an individual and love him after an apparently casual meeting; He could bring something hopeful and good out of a clash of personalities; He could rescue two bent on some collision course and turn disaster into success. We observe this from the accounts of His healing work; He saw through the wounds of the sick to the curing of them. He was as concerned about the spiritual condition of the patient as about His physical handicap or deformity. 'Your sins are forgiven you' becomes a winning phrase; 'your faith has saved you' is a triumphant refrain.

Amid all the defeats and set-backs in a strife-torn community, there have been victories unpublicised but none the less lasting. The phrase 'we are winning' could be applied to those areas which have witnessed a renewal of Christian life and a deeper understanding of the implications of such summings up of the Christian gospel as 'one died for all and therefore all died'. The very word 'community' has come into currency to express the restoration of a neighbourhood after a widespread destruction of houses and homes, as well as the friendly relationships of the occupants. The refusal of a sufferer to show bitterness or vindictiveness when death has struck his family is one of the spiritual victories that gives God the glory. 'Others have suffered more' is a gallant utterance in this kind of situation, 'I must try to help them in their distress, now that the tragedy of it all has been brought home to me through my personal loss'. The loss begins to show gains from this very point of vision. One who has seen some notable spiritual victories in a parish, battered by riot and destruction, has written 'We are always capable of that flash of genius which is forgiveness'.

Likewise, the word 'reconciliation', a term of fundamental significance in the Christian vocabulary, comes to life in a remarkable way when there is apparent defeat, and near-despair of any change or improvement in a grim situation. God was in Christ reconciling the world to Himself. 'The new testament does not speak of God being reconciled to man, but of man being reconciled to God, and of God as the reconciler, taking the initiative in Christ to that end'.* Similarly, love is not that we loved God but that He loved us and sent His Son to be the propitiation for our sins. Perhaps we can agree with one biblical scholar who described this last sentence as the profoundest of all in scripture.

Reconciliation has movement in its meaning. The word pictures for us an interchange and a communication. When Christ came on the world scene, there was a stirring among the affairs of men. A movement followed from one person to another, from one kind of personality to a completely different character, from two extremes to a meeting point, from Christ to sinners.

*God was in Christ, D. M. Baillie, p. 187.

67

To Comfort and Restore

Christian life and work to-day are crammed with paradoxes and apparent contradictions. Solutions to personal problems are found by confronting pride with humility; the snarling criticisms of the scribes and others who objected to Christ's approach to the paralysed sick man pin-pointed the spiritual lessons that emerged from what was superficially a medical and clinical matter. Answers to spiritual problems are given out of the tangle of argument and defiance. The simplicity of the paralytic's response, when obediently he rose up and walked, provided an effective reply to the doubts and murmurings of the bystanders in the wings of this scene of reconciliation. On that occasion, it was the very religion of the objectors that needed converting.

The word of God which the Christian hears at worship clamours for a practical application. Words of faith heal; words of forgiveness, reconcile. They bridge angry silences and bring fluency to the stammering and the inhibited. They supply answers to the questioning and the perplexed: they bring into effectiveness what they promise and suggest.

Where there are differences in a community—and what communicty is completely free from diversity?—there needs to be an interplay of co-operation and competition. As has been said, teams on the sportsfield play both against each other and with each other at one and the same time. In the constantly changing scene of personal and social problems there cannot be satisfactory fixed or tabloid solutions, but there can be a permanent attitude of give-and-take to bring a charitable flexibility into decisions and agreements at every point. Christ was not a law-maker, but His truth was understood in terms of a way and a life.

The protester, like the prophet, for example the prophet Amos, has a pioneering rôle in the work of reconciliation. The trouble caused by wilful separation from God and an ignoring of His ways and commandments needed to be emphasised and brought into the open before a just settlement could be arrived at and those participating could be in a position not to score points off one another, but to ask that God should win them.

In reconciliation, common ground must be sought. Where there is conflict, it is easier to emphasise the differences and to forget how much is shared and held in common. Listening to the other side of the dispute and argument, discussing differences and facing them, becoming more sensitive and aware of other people—their beliefs, feelings and opinions—are all pre-requisites for finding reconciliation in the search after a righteous peace.

When those who have had little contact or communication with each other begin to meet and work together, sharing a common humanity, and seeing no longer the caricature of the other that only fostered hate, they discover kinship and common interest that encourage neighbourly love. There is, in fact, in the very meeting an act of penitence and a triumph of the spiritual. Such penitence opens the way for Christ's victory over the individual who wishes to have a change of heart and intends to lead a new life.

Peace with a difference

Christian peace has always been peace with a difference. Prayers for peace and reconciliation are best coupled with prayers for the necessary conditions that will allow peace to be given. 'There is no peace for the wicked',* nor can there be peace of mind when the conscience is troubled; no freedom to give and receive in conciliatory mood until repentance clears the way for a fresh beginning. 'Your sins are forgiven arise and walk'. The words of Christ revealed his priorities.

If peace comes dropping slow, it is more than likely that the things which make for peace—understanding, spiritual generosity, sympathy and the rest—have been neglected and need revival.

If the course of this world is to be so peaceably ordered that people may joyfully serve, then peace must not only be proclaimed from the house-tops, but also lived in the rooms under the roof and not only lived but demonstrated. It is little use crying 'peace, peace' when there is no peace. This goes for the individual as well as for a whole people: we all have a bent for self-deception and the gift for looking in the wrong direction with the blind or blinkered eye of one who simply won't see.

Peace was left with the Christians after Jesus bade them farewell and was taken up out of their sight. This single word peace was a multiple gift; it included integrity, harmony, justice, fellowship in community and many more of the things that make for wholeness and fullness of life, for 'comfort' and 'restoration'.

These several parts of the single gift formed the good news of victory and salvation. This news was noised abroad through teaching and by preaching, but more than this was required if the meaning of it all was to be made plain and urgent.

Peace must be lived. The Christian faith progressed in a life of community and fellowship that was shared. They lived a common life in the body of Christ. As

*Isaiah 48, 22.

members one of another, these members had not all the same function and character. Faith was found to be not only knowledge, information and instruction, important as the content of faith assuredly is, but it is also shown up in obedience, behaviour and manner. If faith is not in action, it is less than the Christian faith given to people to use and to act upon with drive, confidence and initiative in the midst of the world's concerns.

Doing the will of God and following His commands claimed obedience from every part of the lives of those who received the message of peace. This rather forbidding word 'obedience' asked for no blind adherence to rigid laws. Yet a discipline and order that often make for happiness all in the most trivial of situations and on many light and unimportant social occasions are also to be included in the living conditions of peace.

Peace is not therefore mere absence of war or strife nor yet the stillness of apathy and the sluggishness of inactivity. The winners of peace awards are creative people, sometimes with the might of the pen, at other times with the magnetic imaginativeness of leadership in every sort of human tangle and disaster. If, as has been said, 'development is the modern word for peace', then service, that attractive characteristic of the earliest Christian life, must be the aim of every peace-maker. Jesus was not only called Master and Lord; He himself emphasised the place of service in every part of a ministry which included the discomfort of homelessness, the chores of foot-washing as well as the strain of healing and the pain of sacrificial self-giving. This manner of man was the prince of peace.

Into that small word of calm and quiet serenity He poured all the energy of a dynamic and reconciling love.

In a life of ordered purpose, with the end always in view, the fruits of peace were enjoyed. The price of such a peace lies in the discipline of our giving. In God's will is our peace. The fruit of righteousness is peace.

The washing of the disciples' feet by their master was an acted parable, designed to prepare the members of the inner circle of His friends for the shocks and surprises of a life totally humble and unequivocally committed. The loving and self-giving purpose of Christ's entire life upon earth was demonstrated in terms of water and a basin, a towel and travel-stained feet.

Jesus washed His disciples' feet at Passover-time while supping with them. The air of the room was charged with memories and hidden meaning. Servants were girded with towels, slaves washed their masters' feet; water spelt life and purifying; the Passover recalled a mighty rescue operation and a new-found freedom. The master at the table suddenly became servant to His disciples; the host left His prominent place at the feast where He presided, and stepped down to perform a menial task.

This dramatic gesture illustrated a memorable saying, treasured in the early preaching of the Christian gospel: 'I am among you as one who serves'.* The simple act demonstrated the truth that had been proclaimed at Christ's birth: He was made truly man; becoming man, He was involved in all the limitations human life and accepted them voluntarily and graciously. St. Paul expressed this coming down to man's condition in other ways, when he wrote that Christ emptied himself, counting it not a prize to be equal with God, taking the form of a servant, being made in the likeness of men. The washing of the feet as well as the

*Luke 22, 27.

birth in the Bethlehem stable must have been the picture in his mind as he wrote.

The dignity of service, rather than the process of cleansing, is emphasised here. The feet of the disciples, not their hands or their head, were washed. The feet symbolised the action and movement of those who toiled and travelled. Peter seemed to miss the point when he asked for more than he was offered after his first protest and refusal. The levelling spirit of this gracious condescension linked Christ's incarnation with His crucifixion and provided one more example of His complete identification with the life and lot of men in the world that He had come to serve and save. In an early Irish illuminated service book* feet-washing is included in the rite of baptism. The command was heard by the worshippers after the symbolic act of service and hospitality took place: 'thus do thou to guests and strangers'. Similarly, Maundy ceremonies proclaim the common humanity of monarchs and their subjects, of those who give service to their servants, and find in the passion of Christ a revolution of love and a transvaluation of values.

*Stowe ms.

Chapter 6

Christ above me, Christ beneath me, Christ in quiet

We may wonder how much quiet was to be found in the turbulent days out of which sprang the early Christianity of this country. The island was apparently a place of strife and turmoil—and wild, rugged life. Otherwise, a breastplate would not have been in demand. However, the quiet of silence and the quiet of rest were also present. The appreciation of nature's beauty, the hills, the rivers and the woods is woven into the prayers of those times.

Quiet was sought after as a spiritual treasure. 'Our hearts are unquiet until they find quiet in Thee', wrote Augustine in words that have become famous and familiar, yet never tired or trite. For we all discover the healing properties of rest and quiet in our own lives. There is the stilling of the conscience and the calming of troubled worrying thoughts, the trustfulness that cools down fussiness, the relaxation after tension.

A time off for prayer is a time for withdrawal and retreat before the next advance, a time to gather strength before moving on to new positions. The quiet time provides shelter for a thought or a good resolve that has been sown and now needs some rooting and a chance to develop. Before the winds of distraction and the cold of the world's climate have an opportunity to attack and destroy, a withdrawal, formal or organised, or again private and spontaneous, can give the needed protection. In this way the mind is delivered for a while from the pressures of every-day duties. Off the beaten track, in the hiddenness of prayer and meditation, there is relief from interruptions and a welcome refreshment for the mentally and spiritually exhausted.

In the quiet, we allow ourselves to be regulated by God's time. We hold ourselves in the stillness He gives, ready and open to respond to what He has to say, when other voices are out of earshot and the noises of traffic have died away. We discover that quiet has a creative character. Nothing sluggish is here, no vacuum as abhorrent to God in a personal life as in the work-shop of nature.

Stillness helps us to meet and recognise God. 'Be still and know' we echo from the psalm. One version of that phrase runs: 'have leisure and know'. We owe it to ourselves to find time for God.

Corporate silence is a moving experience. We are prone to talk too much in our praying. We think that we must be heard for our much speaking. The Greeks had a word for silence which paid it a compliment and called it 'good speech'. Silence also has its eloquence.

Helen Waddell has a famous passage in one of her books commending the research in the field of the spiritual carried out by the desert fathers of North Africa. She maintains that specialisation in the realm of prayer is as exacting in standards and discipline as the training and practising carried out by the antarctic explorer as he faces the snow and ice, or again in the trial and testing runs of the racing motorist on the speed track. Although, not perhaps of practical use directly for the ordinary citizen, such experiments in extreme instances and even with eccentric zeal ultimately bring benefits which many non-specialists can share. The findings of pure scholarship and science for all their detailed descriptions and abstruseness become at a later stage available and are welcomed in a far wider world. The calculations, inventions, and the constant search after truth are having their influence all the time. Such is the impact of disinterested research: in the process there are to be found unexpected joys, when skill is exercised for skill's sake.

We all know of examples of eloquent silences. In a bereaved family when death has struck and there seems to be nothing to say, it is important for the friend or counsellor to be there. On a commemoration day that recalls an event which has touched thousands who are of one mind in one place with a single dominating thought; the silence can be felt, almost touched, while all participate in its observance. The event, rather than any words about what is happening, becomes the headline news and impresses all who were present in a way which they will not quickly forget. Few can be left unmoved on such an occasion in the face of the eloquent stillness of minds in tune, with a corporate concentration. One writer has remarked that in Ireland people, generally speaking, have too much imagination to become good pupils or students in the practice of meditation, in the observance of a selected silence.

Silence can be disturbing. It can overwhelm. Some dread the anticipation of a silence, and talk on compulsively. There are also such things as sullen and angry silences, where aloofness prevails and grim misunderstanding brings communication to a grinding halt. Such silences are deafening. People do not trust themselves to speak. Added to this, there are times when any response is unhelpful and the approach of Hezekiah, Judah's king, with his 'answer him not'* is the wisest and most effective. The confrontation of Assyria and Judah provides a parable 'of the everlasting struggle between faith and force'.

The silence that is golden illustrates that there are experiences too deep for words, too deep for tears. A quiet church with its atmosphere of prayer and peace is not to be equated with an empty church; for silence can fill every corner. Nor is a quiet mind an empty, frustrated, baffled mind when facing a predicament or in the eyes of the world cornered and cowed by outside forces of intimidation and superior argument.

Thomas Merton speaks of 'physical solitude, exterior silence, real recollection' as necessary not only as a means to an end, but as a way of growing in love for God and for others.

True Silence

True solitude does not lay an emphasis on an absence of people. It is more like an abyss opening up in the centre of one's being. A hungering and thirsting after righteousness clamour for the filling of the felt gaps.

When we see ourselves with Christ 'above and beneath' us, we find the quiet of space and depth. The 'above' is felt when words fail, when we sense that all the things of which we have been speaking, in discussion and through questioning, taper off into mystery, into the unutterable and the inexpressible. How eloquent

*Isaiah 36, 21.

we recall is 'the rest' marked in the musical score by the composer's genius for contrast and communication. 'Beneath' there is hiddenness, much that is mysterious and unexplored, still puzzling us, left unclear and un-resolved. At times we can only call to God 'out of the deep'. In many a crisis it is only in the depths that we can find Him real and present.

Quiet means stillness and rest. At first, like fasting, quiet has a purpose. It is not an end in itself, but fulfils, as it were, the function of pruning since it stimulates devotion and improves the growth in the life of the spirit. By forfeiting the privilege of speech, silence disciplines both mind and tongue.

Secondly, there is no vacuum in this stillness. Here is a time for listening, not a time to speak. Among the illiterates, St. Patrick found listeners. When books were few and sagas were recited and the bards sang, many listened. In some ways we live, as McLuhan put it, in a post-literate age. Once Martin Luther spoke of words which were visible, understood through the eye-gate and received not through the ear alone. Listening is still one of our needs: we can listen to God through the scriptures, through the drama of the Church's worship and in personal communing with God while at private prayer. We can also hear him in the silences, if we are attuned and ready to give ear.

There was a fanciful tradition that Patrick and his faithful followers were transformed by their faith and prayers so that their enemies did not recognise them. The cry of the deer was heard instead of their human voices. Such was the quaint way of speaking about prayer as protective, used not to ward off some evil eye with the right word to unlock the secret of a spell, but to take to ourselves the power of God. The forgiveness which the penitent experiences rescues him from himself. It helps him to be himself.

Each one of us has a personal wilderness. An untidy corner of the garden holds weeds and rubbish; unless it is there with a function for what we cannot quickly dispose of, we become embarrassed and frustrated. There are wildernesses in our minds as well as on the office desk and in the house-wife's bungalow. In everyone's life, the loose ends of neglect and worry need time for tidying and ordering. It is the same for those who try to pray and serve and to take their place in home, district, city or community.

The voice crying in the wilderness was a voice that was heard. We think of the futility of a lone voice, a minority opinion, but the voice of the prophet preparing the way may not have held vast crowds spellbound but it did have a particular quality and undoubted influence. The actual number of voices chiming in was not of primary importance. The point lay in the truth of his words, the justice of his diagnosis, and his ability to catch the conscience of even a few listeners. John the Baptist, for instance, as the last of a line of prophets, abstained from strong drink but bravely spoke strong words. The wilderness and the solitary place proved a suitable setting for a new programme for living.

Withdrawal is part of the Christian's programme. No feast, without a fast or an appetite or a little hard work, is fully enjoyed by the company at table. Lent is not an end in itself; it is however, an opportunity for training through listening and learning.

It is hard to estimate the importance of silence. Quietness is not achieved by day-dreaming nor by allowing the mind to go blank and lie fallow. It is a matter of relaxation, gained by trusting God, forgetting self, having confidence that He can work in us if we are willing to be dependent, by 'letting go and letting God' in "Loose him and let him go" was said of a humble animal; it becomes a sound piece of advice for a Brother Ass.

The retreat or quiet day has been valued increasingly in days of throbbing traffic and life's background noises and terrors by night. Silence also can terrify; the city dweller is often apprehensive and lonely in the peace of the countryside. Forced to face up to himself with none of the usual accompaniments to buttress him, he thinks in a new way about his relationship to others and his immediate surroundings. Prayer becomes exploration, finding God and allowing God to find him. 'I could not seek thee, hadst thou not already found me' puts the point. There has been too much hiding and dodging. Issues have not been faced. We have not found whom our souls desire to love that we may both find, and be found of, thee'. This is the tone of honest prayer.

Jesus in the wilderness prepared for an intensive ministry of three years, into which period were packed the action and the message that still make their impact in the world He had come to serve and save.

This wilderness-experience underlines the priority of being over doing. To be ourselves, in naked truth and unprotected abandonment is part of self-discovery After we have come to know ourselves, then will follow more easily the right relationships we seek to have with others and, in particular, with those who differ from us in many ways.

To this end the conference house, the community centre, the place of meeting in neighbourhoods where we have roots must be supplemented by the desert place, the quiet sanctuary and places of peace and quiet. Here we can listen to what the spirit says to the churches and in particular to ourselves as members.

To be one's self, to be one's own man is something for Lenten endeavour. To emerge from the family circle and to be away from our own set encourages the ordering and disciplining of our own thinking. This involves self-criticism and a Christian assessment of ourselves and the choices open to us; slogans or short cuts, while pros and cons are weighed, can be of little help. The moral ambiguities of life try and tax our patience and courage with long-term remedies. If at times there is a mirage in the desert, deceiving us with false promises of refreshment, there is also a mirror there in the cool oasis showing us to ourselves as we really are.

Chapter 7

Christ in danger

Every age has its dangerous days. Early Irish Christianity did not escape perils and persecutions. The dangers were both physical and spiritual.

The dangers in the desert by Jordan may have included wild beasts: but the temptations that befell Jesus are the hazards that attract our interest and have most to teach us.

We turn our minds to spiritual dangers: the seven deadly sins were listed in a time of retreat. Pride headed the list and is recognised as the root sin by general consent. 'Pride ruled my will' is a sentence that has echoed many times in genuine self-examination. Self-interest, self-centredness and self-preservation are strong motives influencing the every-day decisions of the individual. How to have a responsibility for self, a true love of self, a self-respect and a self-esteem without becoming either selfish or self-opinionated or self-indulgent is the question mark placed against the Christian's life.

To be aware of the dangers and to cope with the temptations is to be forearmed in this field of behaviour. To be positive, and not merely passive or drifting, amid the pressures of impulses and desires will include concern for others, the seeing of ourselves as others see us, and a sense of dependence, difficult as this may be to acquire, despite our self-reliance and treasured individuality. Above all, the prayer to God for grace, His active love, and His transforming power must be seen as a defence against those dangers, those sins 'that do so easily beset us'.

Avoidance of occasions of temptation may be possible, but there are times when they have to be encountered and cannot be by-passed. Not only avoidance but resistance is required. This resistance can be made with positive antidotes. Good desires overcome unworthy or sordid cravings. Generous service alters the attitude to work and earning that measures all by profit and the money motive. Neighbourliness draws into our private lives those who have their homes near to us. Through this proximity we find life becoming fuller and often richer in outlook. The risks in venturing forth into life with a social responsibility are more acceptable than the dangers that attend the self-contained life, the exclusive line of action, and the narrower vision of private piety.

The Breastplate furnishes us with a living prayer in a dangerous situation. Those who used its words at first felt protected. Not that they had the siege mentality. Here was equipment for the way forward: 'the power of God to hold and lead'.

Sometimes it might appear as if the mention of dangers and adversities, of foes and woes, occurs too frequently with a style overdone in our set forms of prayer, in the words we use and in hymns we sing. On reflection, however, we realise that spiritual dangers are always present and constantly demand our attention through prayer, through resolve and through action.

Complacency, that feeling of self-satisfaction, is one of these constant perils. If we are all right, is that not enough in a world full of impossible and insoluble problems? Or again, if we give some of our goods to feed the poor, if we support famine relief and funds for innocent victims of disaster, is not that something creditable, even more than is required of us? If we feel concern for many things and yet too readily decide that there is little that we can do, only touching the fringe or tinkering with a gigantic breakdown of vast machinery? Tempting questions crop up and, when un-answered, because they seem unanswerable, we slip back into ways that have in them the poison of in-difference and the dope of a decent respectability which covers danger spots and looks away from the trouble and fails to hear the crying need.

A tendency to minimise dangers and difficulties in life shown by those who write books for the very young has been noticed and commented on. To indicate that all is smooth and easy for those growing up and then to allow them at adolescence to plunge into descriptions of the sordid, tangled, violent and crude human experience scarcely prepares the young for life with any realism nor yet with adequate information to protect and guide them. The horror stories of an earlier age that introduced the very young to the fact of death and the perils of vice in a grisly underworld of crime and deceit may have overplayed the drama of life, but for the pendulum to swing in the other direction to a dreamy, fanciful, never-never world, lays the child open to dangers and perils no less than those ever present on the busy road, where the balance has to be kept between over-protection with the encouragement of caution and awareness through instruction and high-way drill.

The battle with disease is being nobly fought and the safe-guards of immunisation have saved countless lives. This freedom from fear in the field of health has brought wonderful happiness and confidence into family life and to all those growing up in the world. Rules of health, of course, have still to be observed. Complete immunity from outbreaks of plagues and epidemics is not expected nor are the dangers to health ignored.

Those who companied with Jesus were certainly not immune from the spiritual dangers that attack every human life. Strange to say, we notice more markedly and with a more stringent criticism the faults of those who have tried to follow Christ and to be with Him. Peter's denial no less than the betrayal of Judas, not to mention the complete disappearance of the chosen disciples 'when they all forsook him and fled' give us a rude shock and contain a salutary warning. It has been said that Jesus revealed the badness of goodness when He denounced the pharisaic attitude: the good had their limitations, holding to the law and every letter of it; yet the dry application of the strict and detailed regulations and the cold approach to people in moral trouble left out important human factors and showed a grave misunderstanding of what life was all about. Through Peter's denial we learn deeper things about his love and the testing of it; we learn also new things about God's forgiveness and His power to build more strongly a character after initial defeat and the ordeal of being broken before the rebuilding. Experience teaches the hard and dangerous way.

The unknown is feared. The sin when recognised and then rejected loses its sting and is the less dangerous. The fear of the unknown overpowers and intimidates; people are afraid to be themselves; they are not free to be themselves; they are often victims of situations in which they had no part: they are in spiritual and often also in physical peril: the opposite of such fear is faith.

Sometimes faith is coupled with fear in the language of Christian prayer. At other times the two are polarised.

The word 'fear' itself has a multiple meaning. There is a godly fear for which we pray when arrogance and haughty pride dominate our motives and enlarge our self-esteem. There is a reverence for life sorely needed in callous, cruel days; such a protective fear of God and His creation keeps us in our place and puts service before acquisitiveness, preferring spirit to space. The fear of the Lord is no cringing reaction to God's might and majesty. It shows healthy respect and due reverence.

The fearing and trembling are experienced in the face of goodness, greatness, and mystery. Jacob awoke from his ladder-dream with a sense of God's presence strong in his nerves and sinews. 'How dreadful is this place'* was his completely honest exclamation; it expressed the contrast between himself and God, and yet it displayed an awareness of his own human relationship with one who was wholly 'other'; someone so different that he could not be described, though certainly he was to be respected and reverenced; and since fear means awe, God was the cause of the trembling. We pray in an ancient, living and pertinent prayer that we may have a perpetual 'fear and love' of

*Genesis 28, 17.

God's holy name.

Love is imparted through the tension of fear and faith. Love is exercised through the mind as well as through the body, through an obedient response of will no less than through the charms of mutual attraction. Perfect love casts out the base fears, displayed when faith fails and nerves collapse and courage crumples.

The 'fear of fears' besets many in our day who are sick, sore and tired of disorders, uncertainties, dangers, terrors, and intimidations. This kind of fear gnaws at a life which has lived within the limits of an even tenor, an unquestioning routine, an unawareness of the world's more formidable predicaments. Such fear, bred of insecurity, must be met by a faith in a future based on trust, fair dealing, personal relationships confidently established with those whose neighbourhood, work and future hopes are shared together. Association, not confrontation; fellowship, instead of cliques; converging interests rather than competitive pursuits; these transformations in society can only emerge from a faith that overcomes fear.

Fear of death and the unknown melts away in the light and warmth of the Christian news of resurrection. Those who were afraid at the time of the first Easter event became renewed and changed people when the evidence banished their ignorance and their misgivings. When God raised Jesus from the dead, the sting was drawn from death. The whole character of this fact of life was altered; death in future was to mean completion, presence, union in fellowship. The fears of great things unknown are cast out of experience by perfect love. The lesser fears that vex us must be seen in the widest context of eternal life and the knowledge of God's universal love.

Chapter 8

Christ in hearts of all that love me

Patrick knew what love meant because he had been harshly exposed to hate. Hate has been described by the Venerable Bede as 'anger grown old'. Patrick met the hostility of those who were enemies of Christ with a faith that became for him both a sword and a shield. God spoke to him through every event.

Patrick tells us of his prayers. Like St. Paul, he was asked by the captain of the ship on which he journeyed to pray for the crew in rough seas. He was seen to be a man of prayer and writes of the hundred prayers he uttered daily. He prayed for the country where he had spent the grim years of childhood and yet he gives us the impression that he did not know a soul there. While abroad on his travels he hears the voice of one Victoricus crying 'Come, holy youth, and walk among us again'. The voice comes to him while he is at his prayers. The way of service opens up for him after his wrestling in prayer. Love is made to leave self and flies towards others. He who prays for others with fervour becomes aware of the love that others give to him.

There was an intensity in Patrick's prayers for the people of the country he was ultimately to serve. This concentration is worth noting. We pray as we love. If we pray to order when, for example, someone has asked us to pray for a friend, we find it hard to bring the full measure of love and concern into this requested intercession. The mind is inclined to move from the name supplied to another one, far better known, whose personality lights up our imagination more vividly. We presume to know any person named to us for prayer, because God knows that person. We learn to be familiar in using the name, because he belongs to the family. We find out more about God and His love through this kind of spiritual intercourse than we could have initially guessed.

C. S. Lewis tells movingly of the help that intercessory prayer had been to him in the days when he was anxiously watching over his dying wife. A friend praying for him had been modest and humble about any help his prayers might have provided; he sent this message to C. S. L. 'I know I am outside; my voice can hardly reach you'. This expression of attempted communication helped more than all the slick words of formal consolation, not to speak of other people's artificial cheerfulness and unwarranted optimism that meant very little and exhibited even less understanding before the great mystery of suffering.

Bonhoeffer illustrated the importance of intercession through his references to those of his contemporaries who had relatively little use for prayer, liturgy and devotional exercises. He pointed out that the Church is called to be present and active for the sake of others. 'The Church', he wrote, 'is her true self only when she exists for humanity. She must take her part in the social life of the world, not lording it over men, but helping and serving the world'. He was surprisingly enough in favour of praying all the psalms, not a mere anthology of that spiritual treasure house; he was opposed to picking and choosing a selection according to mood.

In this kind of prayer we make an approach to others through Christ. We find ourselves influenced by such a contact. We pray to become instruments of God's love, to become available, to keep our minds sensitive and ourselves outreaching. We pray that we may respond to God's initiative and power. We pray primarily for our relationship with God and with others.

Our Lord's prayer for unity in the seventeenth chapter of the Gospel according to St. John has become a model in its petitions for a three-fold objective—holiness, truth, and unity. This prayer comes after the strong line Jesus has taken with His disciples: 'courage, I have conquered the world'. He prays for His friends that they may be kept in God's name (verse 11), preserved from evil (verse 15), and sanctified in the truth (verse 19), that they may be one (verse 21) and have fullness of joy (verse 13).

Praying for unity has helped us to be generous in our wishes and has given us indirect and unexpected help in praying for those who are different from us in their outlook and in the manner of their response. To pray in words that will be understood by those from whom we are divided, to use the opportunity of praying together, rather than to find ourselves praying against each other, to make a distinctive contribution of our own to the stream of prayer—these are the features of prayer for unity. Praying with our own offering of love, of penitence, of new-found discoveries in the faith, we ask the Holy Spirit to accomplish his perfect work.

Praying Together

In prayers that breathe unity, we are right perhaps to refrain from harping all the time on the subject of unity itself to the exclusion of any searching after the conditions of life and behaviour that make for unity. We should also be praying for tolerance, for a willingness to change, for friendship, for courtesy, for an honest review of our beliefs and attitudes. Thus we pray as members of Christ's body, even though we are imperfect members, quarrelsome at times, always sinfully falling short of God's glory, and often plain stupid.

The love of Christ has many dimensions. It is broad and long, deep and high. Its measurements have been eloquently and graphically described in the New Testament letter to the Ephesians.

A shadow of mystery surrounds the expression of love. There is nothing facile in the business of loving. Through wonder and worship an unfolding of the mystery begins for us in life as it is now and will continue hereafter. Thus we seek through involvement in life's tragedies to comprehend 'what is the breadth and length and depth and height' of love. This love is experienced in a life with 'him that is able to do exceeding abundantly above all that we ask or think'.

There is perfection in love and fulness in its content. 'The breadth and length and depth and height' are unknown and yet well-known. Those who enter into the mystery to find its open secrets become aware of the mighty dimensions of this love that passes knowledge.

Love was compared with a temple of abiding worship whose foundations were deeply dug: like a building four-square, beautiful in its proportions, complete in its wholeness. Love, too, was paralleled by wisdom with more than physical dimensions; it reached out in all directions to illuminate and reconcile the problems and questionings of mankind.

Others found the shape of a cross in this love, expressed not in terms of argument, but in the drama and poetry of prayer and meditation. The horizontal and the vertical shaped the cross which extended with its arms outstretched from one end of the world to the other, and reached with its upright branch to the heights above and down to the depths below. If, as St. Augustine mused, there was love in the breadth, hope in the height, patience in the length, and humility in the depth, the whole was an expression of the mystery of a love which included suffering and conflict in its practice and unfolding.

The letter to the Ephesians, which includes this hymn to the praise of love, and this prayer which bids the readers adore, makes mention also of the troubles and tribulations of human weakness and evil days. Its message of love proves applicable to every need and covers the whole of life in all its complexities. It is thus difficult to think of Christian love without the ingredients of compassion and sacrifice as were displayed by the crucified. Such love grapples with life as it is and counts no human problem outside its reach or beyond its concern.

The specialised word 'charity' is not to be dismissed as mere love. There must be the core of faith and the ripening of hope in the product of the love that stems from God and earns that particular name of charity. Love as a general word is frequently ambiguous; it sounds light-weight, too trivial for the sturdy virtue that crowns all virtues. Yet love, in the context of faith and hope, binds man to God and person to person in a covenant that only hate, scepticism and treachery can destroy.

Charity was expressed in every movement, attitude, word and purpose of Jesus Christ. In His life the faith and hope underlying the supreme virtue were to be found in historical events, in human situations, in the tense moments of trial, in the crucifying hours of suffering. He suffered long and was kind; He envied not; He thought no evil; He rejoiced not in iniquity, but rejoiced in the truth; He bore all things, believed all things, endured all things. The classical description of love spoke of a life filled with activity and sacrifice. Charity was seen to be personal through and through. The name of Christ could properly be substituted for the word 'charity or love' in St. Paul's famous hymn on this theme (1 Cor. 13). His nature and His name was love.

Such charity can be minted afresh in a setting of bitterness and prejudice if personal relationships are renewed for future co-operation. By abandoning the fixity of entrenched positions, held nervously and stubbornly from the past, but often now irrelevant, new exercises in the fellowship of community and in the shared interests of humility can create an atmosphere for charity to do her perfect work.

Two-way Love

There is no competition between the love of God and the love of neighbour. Where there is love, there is giving; but there is also the desire to receive. Our Lord loved the unlovely; He gave of His time, His compassion and His strength to those who were in need and superficially unattractive, but He also rejoiced to receive hospitality in unpromising quarters and to welcome gifts from unexpected sources. The entertainment He enjoyed at the publican's table and the graciousness with which He received the woman's gift of precious balm, lavishly outpoured, demonstrated His capacity of loving and being loved.

Love cannot be a one-way process. Even if it is given without the counting of the cost or the seeking of a reward, it demands reception and response for its growth and fulfilment. The hot-house Christian, shut in and self-regarding, who claims to love God, but never seems to love anyone else, is aiming in pagan fashion at an independence and a self-sufficiency which are less than human. Patriotism, in spite of its fierce and burning love for country, can easily lack the love for fellow-countrymen in its mad pursuit of an abstract ideal. Philanthropy, perfectly organised on lines of detached benevolence, can likewise be defective. The word 'love' is not mentioned in the story of the prodigal son, but the father-son, compassionate relationship illustrates love's power and love's humanity more clearly than any treatise or sermon on the subject.

Love at its best means love of God and love of God's creation. The love of God seeks obedience from us; the love of neighbour demands action on our part. The sympathy which we are urged to show towards a brother in pain or a sister in want must be more than an activity of the mind or the imagination; it must become a deep and costly sharing of experience.

Yet love does concern the mind as well as the heart. It is tested by physical attraction, but not only so. Love is tried, and then deepened, after it has passed the test, when fond hearts have minds in tune. Love is set on firm foundations when lovers have other concerns besides their own; when they have interests in common;

when they have a spiritual life which they share; when they are bound together in faith and unanimity by a life of fellowship with the Lord of love. Such are not the superficial manifestations of love. These qualities must be given time to be recognised and opportunity to be rated at their true value.

What a common word is love and yet how many different meanings it bears! Christians find that they cannot probe the mystery of the love which man has for woman unless they are prepared to love God as well. The description of marriage as 'God's holy ordinance' suggests this. Marriage does not concern only the two who wish to be joined together; the God who joins them together is also present and active. Furthermore marriage is a matter for society, for friends and in-laws; it is not just the concern of the spouses who minister it.

Thus the love of God is not a thing apart. It furthers and consolidates the love of husband and wife. Bereft of divine love, the married couple will scarcely appreciate the depth and mystery of love in all its transforming power. Likewise faith in God increases the faith which one partner has in the other. In married life, sustained and enriched by a working faith in God, there is likely to be a clearer vision of the need for a spirit of give and take in the home and elsewhere. For faith enables us to understand the part which forgiveness must play in human relationships. By faith, too, we appreciate the place of authority, obedience and patience in the forging of the life of union.

Marriage is a way of life. The lover has the power to choose this way with a partner, but the onus of decision is laid upon him and her. No marriage is perfect. Each partnership needs the constant help of God's sustaining grace. When a marriage is solemnised in church, the personal private decision uttered freely and deliberately by each party is made public and is caught up into the continuous, unbroken and corporate worship of the Creator.

Attention which at first is fastened on the bridal pair at a wedding is switched from the human scene to the realm of the divine. In Christian marriage the love of the man and his wife is offered to the God to whom they belong. Divine love fortifies and sustains unto their lives' end the marital love mutually given and received.

The famous hymn of love is a pinnacle piece. From its heights on the Sunday before Lent we look out over the forty days with our vision refreshed. St. Paul's masterly analysis gives us inspiration and helps us to see the purpose and point of the spiritual discipline which the season prescribes.

We must not rest content, however, with watching from the mountain-top. 'The more excellent way' has to be trodden as well as viewed admiringly. The beauty of the poem-in-prose about Charity shines through the stark and ugly patches of life which clamour for the restorative powers of this heaven-sent gift. Charity is a very special virtue; it is 'the very bond of peace and of all virtues'. It is not, however, a thing apart. Its power enters life, not least at the growing points.

We can readily understand that the word 'charity' has been more commonly used to describe the fruit rather than the root of this 'love divine, all loves excelling'. A charitable work wins our applause, and long may it continue to do so. Yet the charity from which spring the good deeds we admire must be pondered on for its own sake, lest its deeper meaning escape us and its rich quality be watered down.

Chapter 9

Christ in mouth of friend and stranger

The last clause of St. Patrick's prayer is illustrated in
many scenes of the Christian gospel. It would be a suitable caption for the parable of the Good Samaritan.
That parable shows us all up. It is a story that hurts; it
can never be dismissed as a soothing, pretty tale. 'Friend
and stranger'; the phrase gives us a study in contrasts.
As the characters go by on the road down from Jerusalem to Jericho, we see ourselves in the passing show.
The conventional breaks down and fails miserably; the
unexpected happens. Those best qualified to render
service to their fellow men, the priest and the Levite,
with all their knowledge of the highway code, lose the
spirit of their teaching and hold to the letter. Voluntary aid and human compassion come to the rescue,
thanks to an outsider.

In a well-regulated and carefully administered
society, rules and by-laws can become inflexible and
difficult to apply. Technical hitches hindered the priest
and the Levite from functioning in a neighbourly
fashion at a time of emergency. A compassionate love,
stronger than tradition and custom, burst upon the scene

and produced results immediate and practical. Such love was revolutionary but did not actually foster lawlessness or cause chaos. It displayed a genius for interpreting the laws of human behaviour with a fulness and a tenderness that refused to be curbed or frozen.

The Good Samaritan who travelled along the road of accident, disaster and affliction is the outsider, the great stranger. With an unprejudiced, perhaps uneducated eye, he sees the situation which demands his presence; he asks no questions; he makes no preliminary skirmishes to investigate the case. He becomes, in fact as well as by circumstances, a neighbour. Himself a stranger accustomed to opposition and often deprived of sympathy, he knows something of the dangers of the road. Indeed he who told this parable of high-way robbery was also a great stranger. As an outsider, in a spirit of detached concern, often with nowhere to lay his head at night, Jesus was struck forcibly by the hollowness of the rules of society and the hypocrisy of life's conventions. Jesus came upon the scene with good news for bad times; with stirring rebukes for complacent persons and sham characters. The persons in the parable with their contrasting reactions to a human predicament give us a clearer understanding of the meaning of neighbourliness.

Loving a neighbour requires more effort than we suppose. It is true that he is one who lives close by; but he is outside the family circle and he has not been chosen by us as a friend. The neighbour accordingly is someone who is admittedly different in outlook, tastes, and traditions; he may very well not be one to whom we are instinctively drawn. Yet he belongs to our street and our district and is called neighbour. It has been said that in a sense everyone is a neighbour in proportion to the need he has of you. This learning to love people who are unlike ourselves becomes a fundamental lesson in Christian life. Only by such realistic love, which gives service and makes no demands in return, can families avoid the feuds that beset Cain and Abel. Neighbourliness, too, has to be learned by nations of utterly diverse traditions if they wish to live in a relationship of harmony and understanding. By learning to love the other person as oneself and understanding the differences, superficial romance can be turned into a solid, happy marriage. So Saint Patrick prayed that Christ might be in the mouth of friend and stranger. In his loneliness he was called upon to say difficult things and to face unpopularity. One of his duties was to write in stern tones that letter rebuking the Coroticus gang for their persecuting ways. At times, Patrick's friends appear to have been fair-weather figures. He speaks of his own familiar friend in whom he trusted and laments that this was the very one who let him down by betraying a confidence. At other times strangers helped him where friends seemed to fail. He found, however, in every encounter an event which could be used by God for His glory.

As we approach the close of the Lenten season, we discover that all human problems are brought before our eyes in Holy Week. If the events we commemorate happened 'once upon a time', the human reactions of all who were in touch with Jesus and the personal conflicts have an entirely modern ring. We recognise in the crowd scenes no less than in the dilemmas confronting the leading characters of this greatest of all dramas, the very familiar features of to-day's public and private life.

We learn through event rather than through theory.

Lasting truths are conveyed in terms of persons and actions. Philosophising is less in place as we view the happenings that culminated in a crucifixion. Poetry and painting have helped to interpret for us much that remains essentially mysterious. Evie Hone's famous Eton College window depicted the arms of the Cross, generously elongated and sympathetically stretched to include in its embrace all sorts and conditions who sheltered in its shade and found themselves drawn to the crucified one. So the whole person, not only with intellect or emotion, but with a lavish self-giving is compelled to join the scene dominated by the Cross.

The foolishness of all is found to show forth God's wisdom. The joy and the woe, the suffering and the rehabilitation, the defeat and the triumph are strangely partnered in this experience. Opposites are found to be in fellowship. Conflicts no longer destroy; they create new life.

Friend and stranger are drawn into this scene. Life through death in Holy Week reveals life's purpose and life's dimensions. There are those that kill the body, and, after that, have no more that they can do. A life offered fills other lives with hope and courage; an endless life has limitless capacities. Love through suffering deepens human sympathy and strengthens everyman's ability to give generous service to others and to have greater concern for all, without distinction of class, colour, or creed.

The Way of the Cross

The Way of the Cross is the way of light. So runs the old saying, *via crucis via lucis*. Yet on the threshold of Holy Week we peer into the shadows. Darkness rather than light shrouds the events that lead to the crucifixion.

Denial, betrayal, and intrigue fill the pages of the diary of the week. Spies, informers, lurking figures fill the corners of the well-known scenes, emerging from the wings to dominate the stage. Christ in mouth of friend and stranger seems to have a silent role in the greatest drama ever staged. At each point in the progress of the story of the Cross, the world frowns upon God and says 'no' to His will and His call.

At first, we are inclined to dwell exclusively upon the terrible events of this week of all weeks. The cruel nails, the crown of thorns, the mocking and the scourging are symbols of the suffering; they indicate the reality of what occurred and the bitterness of the personal agony. We dare not pass them by, unremembered. This would be callous and unfeeling of us.

Yet there is another approach to all that occurred. As we read the four accounts of the Passion in the narratives of the evangelists, it becomes clear that, amid the moral confusion and active hostility, Christ is serenely and effectively in control of events. He does not merely submit to suffering and injustice; He deals with them. His positive attitude of courage, consistent patience, and calm control makes the way of the Cross a way of healing and reconciliation; along the route human problems have light shed upon them; after the darkness there is bright victory.

We know, often too well, that although suffering may teach us lessons in living and make us wiser, if sadder, people, the very pain and physical discomfort can limit our outlook pathetically, and leave our nature warped and twisted. Such suffering, as an aching tooth causes, may bring depression and distortions into our thinking and habits, when we submit and often succumb to the pain. We lose initiative and control. On the other hand, the consciously accepted suffering of our Lord at His trial and in His passion shed fresh light upon the darkness of the world in which He chose to be involved. Called to suffer, He committed His whole self to the work which He had been given to do.

The way of committal is the path that Christians are summoned to tread to-day. It is a way of light, not darkness. The light shines back from the Easter dawn upon the Crucifixion scene. The Resurrection reversed the pessimism and the denials of the world that sentenced Christ to death.

The message at the other end of the week is God's 'yes' to life; His 'yes' to order, to purpose, to meaning in His world. Oscar Cullmann has used an illustration from the second world war to explain the nature of the victory of the Cross. The decisive battle has been won already on the first Good Friday; D-day is over. There is yet to be a V-day and the struggle goes on. God's victory is over and unquestioned; we continue with the battle against the dark things. But ours is a way of light. As in many other things, so in our victoriousness, we must 'become what we are'—more than conquerors through him that loved us.

As Christ took the initiative at His entry on Palm Sunday, so God in Christ begins things in us still. In a detached mood, we could read of the Cross as a sordid tragedy; committed to its message, we can discover that it lights up our hearts and minds—and also our world. As John Donne expressed it 'The whole life of Christ was a continual passion . . . . His birth and His death were but one continual act, and His Christmas-day and His Good-Friday are but the evening and morning of one and the same day'.

One stranger's friend

That alabaster box, as foretold, became a talking point and still continues to be such, in Christian circles throughout the world, 'wherever the gospel is preached'.*

In a sense, this woman was the stranger's friend and she herself a stranger became through her action a faithful friend. The action spoke eloquently of one person's capacity for love and sacrifice, when the occasion demanded. The homely and intimate gesture of pouring out the ointment unveiled something of life's mystery. Wise sayings and moving sermons have long been forgotten, while this spontaneous offering has made a deep and lasting impression in our own day.

The woman gave of her best without counting the cost. Her gift is linked with Jesus's giving of His life for the world. The bystanders received a new slant on giving; though they did not know it, they were being prepared indirectly for the greatest sacrifice of all time.

Our Lord had praised the widow who threw in her mites to swell the collection at the Temple door; they had meant more than all the wealthier contributions. This gift of ointment found further commendation; its value was incalculable. Love and worship, loyalty and devotion, more precious than any money, are given freely with an unparalleled generosity.

She gave of her best, almost recklessly, because she perceived who he was. Without words, she proclaimed the Saviour, by whose aid, though we may have nothing, we are able to possess everything. She pointed to the Messiah, the anointed King, the Christ, who came to bring good news to the poor, to bind up the brokenhearted and to heal the bruised. The presence of this

*Mark 14, 9.

master of things drew people to him, both friends and strangers, with a magnetic power. Such personal encounters extracted from them their very best.

The woman gave away the ointment, knowing it was the best and most highly valued possession that she had. It may not have appeared a particularly lavish gift; the whole incident must have seemed in the eyes of some a useless demonstration. Others were disgusted at the waste of good ointment and scoffed at the futility of what was taking place. She, however, gave what she had; she did what she could. The love behind the gift made her offering remarkable for reasons that she herself could hardly have guessed.

The ointment was presumably intended for some other purpose. Perhaps she was bringing this costly offering to the Temple, as the custom was; perhaps she was on her way to a funeral; or to a grave in honour of a loved one. Something prompted her to change her mind, to give what she had brought to someone else. The love for her Lord caused her, without calculating on the future or hesitating over the practical wisdom of her intention, to break the box and pour the ointment on His head. His love would go on making demands on this scale.

Christ's strange work

The Cross is the theme of Holy Week and every week. The dead wood of crucifixion was pictured mysteriously and movingly in the minds of believers as a living tree. The events which culminated in the death of Jesus ended not in an abrupt finish but in a lasting fulfilment. So worshippers everywhere think upon the Cross each Good Friday and find in it the meaning of their immediate surroundings. They turn to its crucial message for a solution of their private and local problems. 'All pathways by His feet are worn' wrote the poet,* 'His crown of thorns is every thorn. His cross is is every tree'.

Christians at worship have the opportunity of hearing the several narratives that record the Passion and the Crucifixion. The four evangelists interpret the single, historical incident. Musical composers convey the many messages of the central tragedy to the hearts of their listeners. The Matthew Passion bids us see destiny in the smallest details of the drama. Those who are drawn into the action, are seen to have responsibility, full or diminished, for the trend of events.

Judgment hangs over the human story of betrayal and denial, of blind indifference and culpable ignorance. Some say that man's failure brought God's blessing. Others through the very sufferings learn more of the love of God. Prophecy is fulfilled and purpose is traced through the tangled path of self-deceit and dark envy.

St. Mark's account of the way of the Cross is stark and realistic. Facts are bare facts; they have a horrifying eloquence of their own and compel the listener to sit down before them and be judged, and then to stand up and be counted. There is no escape from the shadow of the Cross. It stretches across the world. It is an international event. It speaks to all races and cultures, to male and female, to bond and free.

The passion according to Saint Luke is painted in the warm colours of compassion. There is tenderness in the terror. There is creativeness in the suffering. The life of Jesus is offered, rather than destroyed. The work He came to do is not defeated nor frustrated by His

*J. M. Plunkett.

capture and death.

Even as He hangs on the Cross, He forgives. Those who do not seem to deserve it come within the scope of His forgiveness. Everyone, be he thief or accomplice, is in some way a hope of God; all have human nature upon which divine grace can work. The rebellious and disobedient throw more light on God's love than anything that apathetic and colourless characters can reflect.

The Fourth Gospel, according to St. John, conveys in its telling a sense of victory through the tale of condemnation and the sentence of death. There is a streak of glory flashing across the story of the Cross. The Passion seems to provide its own argument and stands in no need of human defence. 'This is the Lord's doing and it is wonderful in our eyes'. The last word of the dying Lord 'It is finished' turns out to be an introduction. For finishing is a summing up of an achievement; the results of it followed and have been long and lasting.

No Longer Strangers After Easter

The Easter message extends over the whole of life. Men and women as individuals and also as members of society find stability and vision in this new life.

The experience of the resurrection brought hope and a sense of belonging to those who had been bewildered and blindly fatalistic. No longer did death mean the blank wall that blocked progress at the end of a dark tunnel. The character of death had been altered for those who shared the life of Him who had destroyed death by His own death.

The faithful few who captured the vision of the risen Christ found life no longer lonely, no longer aimless. They felt strangely at home in a world that had been radically altered for those who had found a future and a destiny in the most trivial of incidents. This fellowship, this solidarity of membership in a new-found community became one of the wonders of the resurrection experience.

Those who made their way along to the village of Emmaus, until the day drew in at evening time, felt joy and relaxation in their hearts at one and the same time. They had, in more senses than one, reached a destination when they invited the stranger to share their supper. The stranger was no longer a stranger, when bread was broken and the vision of the Christ was granted to them. This abiding presence changed their lives and made sense of all the questionings and perplexities which preceded that moment of truth. 'Their eyes were opened and they knew him'.

Christians have often been described as people who lived 'in Christ'. The phrase sounds simple; its meaning is profound. 'Dwelling in Christ' describes their status and indicates the fulfilment of their existence. Strangers, who had no abiding city, and were written off as displaced persons discovered themselves when they became incorporated in the life of their Lord. At first they followed Christ, striving to imitate His ways and obey His teaching; later they became identified with Him.

Pilgrims, who had journeyed with a spiritual search-party, reached a resting-place. Here they found relaxation but not emptiness. The resting-place was the scene, not of idleness, but of fresh life and true re-creation.

Thus the resurrection of Christ confronted those who responded to the event, not with an instant shock, but in lives that experienced the touch, the words, the presence of their Master and found that all their doubts and embarrassments had been turned into solid truth. Such truth had come to stay. No longer strangers and pilgrims, they were citizens with responsibilities and rights in a life of endless promise.

The practising Christian is constantly faced with the difficulty of extending his love and concern to those who do not belong to his own group, his own set, to those who are not in the intimate fellowship of his own communion.

Yet Christians are committed to serving the world. There is no place for exclusiveness, bigotry, racism, unfair discriminations, for God so loved the world that He gave His son.

The differing Churches surely share an attitude towards the stranger. In the ten commandments there is concern for the stranger 'within your gates'. Churches are called to come into a living and creative relationship with one another. To have a relationship that is marked by firm, sincere convictions and a knowledge of the reasons for the faith that is in us is to cast off the defensive spirit and to emerge from immaturity. Jesus called people to change, to be new persons; in this way He freed their hearts from restrictions and brought an end to the half-truths which imprisoned them. As has been well said of our life in community: 'we need a new birth characterised by love, forgiveness and service rather than by harshness and separateness'.

We often find ourselves falling into the trap of over-simplifying life and clinging over-emotionally to slogans, without considering the words we repeat in the light of our own prayer and discussion. We deceive ourselves even when we admit that we are not perfect and we often project our own faults upon others. Words of bitterness, intolerance, and spiritual pride break up society and foster suspicions. Thus estrangement sets in and leads us to express the faith we hold dear in negative and controversial terms. "Hate," in the words of Anthony Bloom "sees a caricature of a man. Love sees his sonship. Hatred looks for means of destruction. Love seeks and finds the pure stream of water at the heart of the polluted river. There is an element of death in love, a dying to self, a living for others even to the ultimate sacrifice."

We are thankful for any effort made to find Christ in stranger as well as in friend. 'If we love those who like us, what thank have we?' But to love a person who is different involves a change in attitude, a widening of interest and an extension of our programme of activities.

The call to make sacrifices comes in here. Sacrifice has two meanings: a loss and an offering. The Christian emphasis rests not on our loss but on another's gain. Thus we can find joy in unexpected places. Anthony Bloom helps us further in this: 'A woman does not talk about the ceaseless care given to her child, night and day, as sacrifice,' he writes, 'she gives herself in joyous love to the needs of her child. Whatever sacrifice we make for God's sake to His children is our response to Him in joy, in gratitude, and in love.'

'Christ in mouth of friend and stranger' is a prayer not alone for Lent but for life. So we seek a balance in the unexpected contrasts of living, interweaving things of the mind and things of the senses, suggesting the most remote things by the simplest and most familiar. 'This' wrote Margaret Cunningham, 'gives us a directness we rejoice in—for example, the *Breastplate* with its wild cry of desire and comprehension'.

Questions for discussion

Chapter 1

1. What, for the Christian, makes a good Lent?
2. Discuss the possibilities of special days of prayer in a community.
3. How can we make progress in praying?

Chapter 2

1. What are the distinctive features of Christian prayer and worship?
2. What can we learn for living today from the spiritual experiences of St. Patrick's time?
3. To how many occupations and professions can we properly apply the description 'vocation'?

Chapter 3

1. What lessons can we learn from the history of our faith?
2. How far is the distinction made between a 'problem' and a 'mystery' in this chapter a valid one?
3. What do we hope for when we pray for peace?

Chapter 4

1. In what ways can our observance of Lent help other people?
2. How can a Christian through prayer turn a worry into a concern? How can the Christian make sense of the phrase 'be not anxious'?
3. What may we pray for in our intercessions?

Chapter 5

1. How can one begin to pray again after long neglect and indifference?
2. What is meant by reconciliation in a family or community?
3. Why is the spirit of forgiveness and repentance counted as essential for Christian living and action?

Chapter 6

1. What is the purpose of withdrawing from some of our usual routine in Lent?
2. How far do the words of other people's prayers help us when we try to pray?
3. Why do some dread silence or a time of quiet?

Chapter 7

1. What are the chief causes for fears in any community?
2. How can a Christian deal with individual fears?
3. Why is complacency a dangerous spiritual condition?

Chapter 8

1. Why should I love God?
2. How many different meanings for the word 'love' occur in our speech and thought?

3. To what does the commandment 'love your neighbour' commit us?

Chapter 9

1. What have the dramatic events, recalled in Holy Week, to do with us today?
2. How can the way of the Cross be the way of light?
3. In what new ways can the spirit and example of the parable of the Good Samaritan be brought into those areas of our lives together where there is a need of healing, caring and reconciling?

Appendix

Two other versions of the 'Christ be with me' stanza

Christ with me, Christ before me, Christ behind me,
Christ in me, Christ beneath me, Christ above me,
Christ on my right, Christ on my left,
Christ where I lie, Christ where I sit, Christ where I
arise,
Christ in the heart of every man who thinks of me,
Christ in the mouth of every man who speaks of me,
Christ in every eye that sees me,
Christ in every ear that hears me.

Translated by L. Bieler, 1953
(after W. Stokes and J. Strachan, 1903)

Christ near
Christ here
Christ be with me
Christ beneath me
Christ within me
Christ behind me
Christ be o'er me
Christ before me
Christ on the left and the right
Christ hither and thither
Christ in the sight
Of each eye that shall seek me
Christ in each ear that shall hear
Christ in each mouth that shall speak me
Christ not the less
In each heart I address.

Translated by George Sigerson, 1907
(The Christian Dawn: the Guardsman's cry)

ACKNOWLEDGMENTS

Grateful acknowledgment is made to SCM Press for the quotation of Dietrich Bonhoeffer from *Letters and Papers from Prison*, SCM Press 1971; to the Oxford University Press and Cambridge University Press for quotations from the *New English Bible*; and to the Division of Education of the National Council of Churches of Christ in the USA for quotations from the *Revised Standard Version*; to Dr Ludwig Bieler for permission to use his version of Christ be with me. And to the Irish Times where a number of these ideas first appeared.